Clinical Rotation Companion

Published May 2024.

ISBN: 978-1-959539-12-4

Published by Kai Land Press LLC
Atlanta, GA

For permissions contact kailandpress@gmail.com

This Clinical Rotation Companion belongs to:

SKILLS	DATE PERFORMED

CLINICAL ROTATION	SEMESTER	FACILITY	INSTRUCTOR

REMEMBER THIS!!!

ADULT VITAL SIGNS

- Heart rate: 60-100 bpm
- Respirations: 12-18 bpm
- Blood pressure: sys 90-120/diast 60-80
- Temperature: 97.5°F-99.1°F (36.4°C-37.3°C)
- SpO2: 95%-100%

COMPLETE BLOOD COUNT (CBC)

- WBC: 4,500-10,000
- RBC: Male-4.3-5.9 Female-3.5-5.5
- Hemoglobin (Hgb): Male-13.5-17.5 Female-12-16
- Hematocrit (Hct): Male-41-53 Female-36-46
- Platelets (Plt): 150,000-400,000

COMMON CONVERSIONS

- 1000 micrograms (mcg)= 1 milligram (mg)
- 1000 milligrams (mg)= 1 gram (g)
- 1000 grams (g)= 1 kilogram (kg)
- 1000 milliliters (mL)= 1 liter (L)
- 1 milliliter (mL)= 1 cubic centimeter (cc)
- 5 milliliters (mL)= 1 teaspoon (tsp)
- 15 milliliters (mL)= 1 tablespoon (tbsp)
- 30 milliliters (mL)= 1 ounce (oz)
- 3 teaspoon (tsp)= 1 tablespoon (tbsp)
- 2 tablespoons (tbsp)= 1 ounce (oz)
- 2.2 pounds (lb)= 1 kilogram (kg)

COMP. METABOLIC PANEL (CMP)

- Glucose: 70-100 mg/dL
- Sodium: 135-145 mEq/L
- Potassium: 3.5-5.1 mEq/L
- Magnesium: 1.5-2.5 mEq/L
- Calcium: 8.5-10.2 mg/dL
- Chloride: 96-106 mEq/L
- CO2: 23-29 mEq/L
- Creatinine: 0.6 to 1.3 mg/dL
- BUN: 6-20 mg/dL
- Albumin: 3.4-5.4 g/dL
- Alkaline phosphatase: 20-130 U/L
- ALT: 4-36 U/L
- AST: 8-33 U/L
- Total bilirubin: 0.1-1.2 mg/dL
- Total protein: 6.0-8.3 g/dL

1. ASK QUESTIONS! ALWAYS CLARIFY!
2. Prepare as much as possible before or at the start of your shift.
3. Plan your day.
4. Be eager to learn.
5. Volunteer to see procedures and try out skills.
6. Practice knowing the brand and generic names of drugs.
7. Write down codes for rooms and doors.
8. Be clear about what you can and can't do as a student nurse during each rotation according to each facility.
9. Treat each clinical site and rotation as a potential pre-interview for job placement post-graduation. Many nurses start their careers at sites used during clinical rotations.
10. ABC's- Airway, Breathing, Circulation

HEAD-TO-TOE ASSESSMENT TIPS

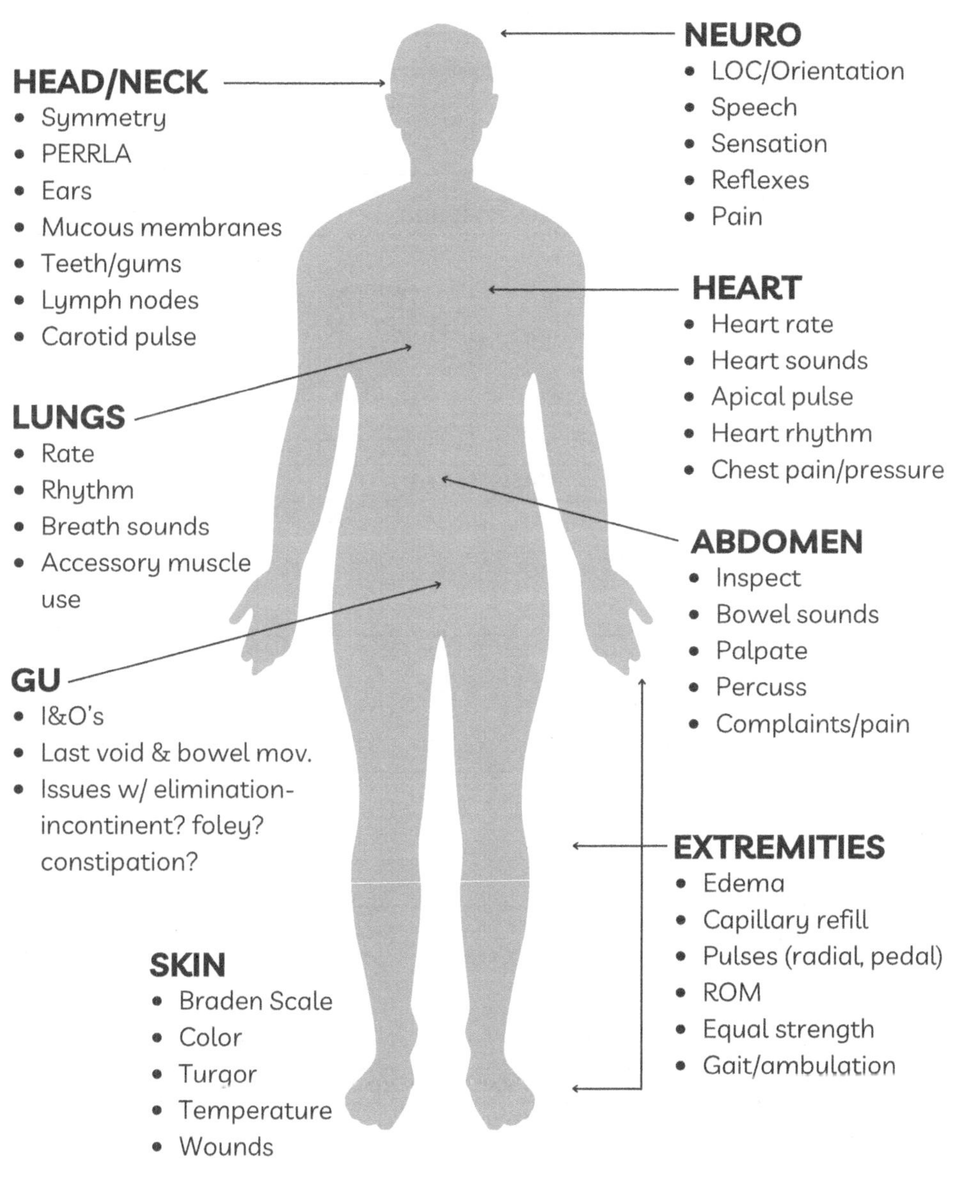

SBAR (PATIENT OVERVIEW)

SITUATION

ROOM NAME AGE/SEX CODE ADMIT DATE	DIAGNOSIS MD/CONSULTS ALLERGIES

BACKGROUND

MEDICAL HISTORY	FALL RISK PRECAUTIONS ISOLATION DIET IV & SITE

ASSESSMENT

VITALS	NEURO	RESP
	CARDIO	GI
	GU	MUSCULOSKELETAL
Na / Glucose K / WBC Mg / Hgb Ca / Hct Ph / Plt Cr / PT/INR BUN / Other	SKIN	PSYCH

RECOMMENDATIONS

PLAN OF CARE	TO-DO LIST	PATIENT EDUCATION

MEDICATION LIST

GENERIC NAME: **BRAND NAME:**
DOSE: ROUTE: DRUG CLASS:
INDICATION(S): NOTES:

GENERIC NAME: **BRAND NAME:**
DOSE: ROUTE: DRUG CLASS:
INDICATION(S): NOTES:

GENERIC NAME: **BRAND NAME:**
DOSE: ROUTE: DRUG CLASS:
INDICATION(S): NOTES:

GENERIC NAME: **BRAND NAME:**
DOSE: ROUTE: DRUG CLASS:
INDICATION(S): NOTES:

GENERIC NAME: **BRAND NAME:**
DOSE: ROUTE: DRUG CLASS:
INDICATION(S): NOTES:

GENERIC NAME: **BRAND NAME:**
DOSE: ROUTE: DRUG CLASS:
INDICATION(S): NOTES:

GENERIC NAME: **BRAND NAME:**
DOSE: ROUTE: DRUG CLASS:
INDICATION(S): NOTES:

GENERIC NAME: **BRAND NAME:**
DOSE: ROUTE: DRUG CLASS:
INDICATION(S): NOTES:

GENERIC NAME: **BRAND NAME:**
DOSE: ROUTE: DRUG CLASS:
INDICATION(S): NOTES:

GENERIC NAME: **BRAND NAME:**
DOSE: ROUTE: DRUG CLASS:
INDICATION(S): NOTES:

GENERIC NAME: **BRAND NAME:**
DOSE: ROUTE: DRUG CLASS:
INDICATION(S): NOTES:

GENERIC NAME: **BRAND NAME:**
DOSE: ROUTE: DRUG CLASS:
INDICATION(S): NOTES:

CARE PLAN

ASSESSMENT

SUBJECTIVE DATA:

OBJECTIVE DATA:

NURSING DIAGNOSIS

PROBLEM(S):

ETIOLOGY:

SIGNS AND SYMPTOMS:

PLANNING

GOAL:

DESIRED (MEASURABLE) OUTCOME:

IMPLEMENTATION

INTERVENTIONS:

EVALUATION

OUTCOME:

EVIDENCED BY:

NOTES

SBAR (PATIENT OVERVIEW)

SITUATION	
ROOM NAME AGE/SEX CODE ADMIT DATE	DIAGNOSIS MD/CONSULTS ALLERGIES

BACKGROUND	
MEDICAL HISTORY	FALL RISK PRECAUTIONS ISOLATION DIET IV & SITE

ASSESSMENT			
VITALS		NEURO	RESP
		CARDIO	GI
		GU	MUSCULOSKELETAL
Na K Mg Ca Ph Cr BUN	Glucose WBC Hgb Hct Plt PT/INR Other	SKIN	PSYCH

RECOMMENDATIONS		
PLAN OF CARE	TO-DO LIST	PATIENT EDUCATION

MEDICATION LIST

GENERIC NAME: **BRAND NAME:**
DOSE: ROUTE: DRUG CLASS:
INDICATION(S): NOTES:

GENERIC NAME: **BRAND NAME:**
DOSE: ROUTE: DRUG CLASS:
INDICATION(S): NOTES:

GENERIC NAME: **BRAND NAME:**
DOSE: ROUTE: DRUG CLASS:
INDICATION(S): NOTES:

GENERIC NAME: **BRAND NAME:**
DOSE: ROUTE: DRUG CLASS:
INDICATION(S): NOTES:

GENERIC NAME: **BRAND NAME:**
DOSE: ROUTE: DRUG CLASS:
INDICATION(S): NOTES:

GENERIC NAME: **BRAND NAME:**
DOSE: ROUTE: DRUG CLASS:
INDICATION(S): NOTES:

GENERIC NAME: **BRAND NAME:**
DOSE: ROUTE: DRUG CLASS:
INDICATION(S): NOTES:

GENERIC NAME: **BRAND NAME:**
DOSE: ROUTE: DRUG CLASS:
INDICATION(S): NOTES:

GENERIC NAME: **BRAND NAME:**
DOSE: ROUTE: DRUG CLASS:
INDICATION(S): NOTES:

GENERIC NAME: **BRAND NAME:**
DOSE: ROUTE: DRUG CLASS:
INDICATION(S): NOTES:

GENERIC NAME: **BRAND NAME:**
DOSE: ROUTE: DRUG CLASS:
INDICATION(S): NOTES:

GENERIC NAME: **BRAND NAME:**
DOSE: ROUTE: DRUG CLASS:
INDICATION(S): NOTES:

CARE PLAN

ASSESSMENT

SUBJECTIVE DATA:

OBJECTIVE DATA:

NURSING DIAGNOSIS

PROBLEM(S):

ETIOLOGY:

SIGNS AND SYMPTOMS:

PLANNING

GOAL:

DESIRED (MEASURABLE) OUTCOME:

IMPLEMENTATION

INTERVENTIONS:

EVALUATION

OUTCOME:

EVIDENCED BY:

NOTES

SBAR (PATIENT OVERVIEW)

SITUATION

ROOM NAME AGE/SEX CODE ADMIT DATE	DIAGNOSIS MD/CONSULTS ALLERGIES

BACKGROUND

MEDICAL HISTORY	FALL RISK PRECAUTIONS ISOLATION DIET IV & SITE

ASSESSMENT

VITALS	NEURO	RESP
	CARDIO	GI
	GU	MUSCULOSKELETAL
Na / Glucose K / WBC Mg / Hgb Ca / Hct Ph / Plt Cr / PT/INR BUN / Other	SKIN	PSYCH

RECOMMENDATIONS

PLAN OF CARE	TO-DO LIST	PATIENT EDUCATION

MEDICATION LIST

GENERIC NAME:		BRAND NAME:
DOSE:	ROUTE:	DRUG CLASS:
INDICATION(S):	NOTES:	
GENERIC NAME:		**BRAND NAME:**
DOSE:	ROUTE:	DRUG CLASS:
INDICATION(S):	NOTES:	
GENERIC NAME:		**BRAND NAME:**
DOSE:	ROUTE:	DRUG CLASS:
INDICATION(S):	NOTES:	
GENERIC NAME:		**BRAND NAME:**
DOSE:	ROUTE:	DRUG CLASS:
INDICATION(S):	NOTES:	
GENERIC NAME:		**BRAND NAME:**
DOSE:	ROUTE:	DRUG CLASS:
INDICATION(S):	NOTES:	
GENERIC NAME:		**BRAND NAME:**
DOSE:	ROUTE:	DRUG CLASS:
INDICATION(S):	NOTES:	
GENERIC NAME:		**BRAND NAME:**
DOSE:	ROUTE:	DRUG CLASS:
INDICATION(S):	NOTES:	
GENERIC NAME:		**BRAND NAME:**
DOSE:	ROUTE:	DRUG CLASS:
INDICATION(S):	NOTES:	
GENERIC NAME:		**BRAND NAME:**
DOSE:	ROUTE:	DRUG CLASS:
INDICATION(S):	NOTES:	
GENERIC NAME:		**BRAND NAME:**
DOSE:	ROUTE:	DRUG CLASS:
INDICATION(S):	NOTES:	
GENERIC NAME:		**BRAND NAME:**
DOSE:	ROUTE:	DRUG CLASS:
INDICATION(S):	NOTES:	
GENERIC NAME:		**BRAND NAME:**
DOSE:	ROUTE:	DRUG CLASS:
INDICATION(S):	NOTES:	

CARE PLAN

ASSESSMENT

SUBJECTIVE DATA:

OBJECTIVE DATA:

NURSING DIAGNOSIS

PROBLEM(S):

ETIOLOGY:

SIGNS AND SYMPTOMS:

PLANNING

GOAL:

DESIRED (MEASURABLE) OUTCOME:

IMPLEMENTATION

INTERVENTIONS:

EVALUATION

OUTCOME:

EVIDENCED BY:

NOTES

SBAR (PATIENT OVERVIEW)

SITUATION

ROOM NAME AGE/SEX CODE ADMIT DATE	DIAGNOSIS MD/CONSULTS ALLERGIES

BACKGROUND

MEDICAL HISTORY	FALL RISK PRECAUTIONS ISOLATION DIET IV & SITE

ASSESSMENT

VITALS	NEURO	RESP
	CARDIO	GI
	GU	MUSCULOSKELETAL
Na Glucose K WBC Mg Hgb Ca Hct Ph Plt Cr PT/INR BUN Other	SKIN	PSYCH

RECOMMENDATIONS

PLAN OF CARE	TO-DO LIST	PATIENT EDUCATION

MEDICATION LIST

GENERIC NAME:		BRAND NAME:
DOSE:	ROUTE:	DRUG CLASS:
INDICATION(S):	NOTES:	
GENERIC NAME:		BRAND NAME:
DOSE:	ROUTE:	DRUG CLASS:
INDICATION(S):	NOTES:	
GENERIC NAME:		BRAND NAME:
DOSE:	ROUTE:	DRUG CLASS:
INDICATION(S):	NOTES:	
GENERIC NAME:		BRAND NAME:
DOSE:	ROUTE:	DRUG CLASS:
INDICATION(S):	NOTES:	
GENERIC NAME:		BRAND NAME:
DOSE:	ROUTE:	DRUG CLASS:
INDICATION(S):	NOTES:	
GENERIC NAME:		BRAND NAME:
DOSE:	ROUTE:	DRUG CLASS:
INDICATION(S):	NOTES:	
GENERIC NAME:		BRAND NAME:
DOSE:	ROUTE:	DRUG CLASS:
INDICATION(S):	NOTES:	
GENERIC NAME:		BRAND NAME:
DOSE:	ROUTE:	DRUG CLASS:
INDICATION(S):	NOTES:	
GENERIC NAME:		BRAND NAME:
DOSE:	ROUTE:	DRUG CLASS:
INDICATION(S):	NOTES:	
GENERIC NAME:		BRAND NAME:
DOSE:	ROUTE:	DRUG CLASS:
INDICATION(S):	NOTES:	
GENERIC NAME:		BRAND NAME:
DOSE:	ROUTE:	DRUG CLASS:
INDICATION(S):	NOTES:	
GENERIC NAME:		BRAND NAME:
DOSE:	ROUTE:	DRUG CLASS:
INDICATION(S):	NOTES:	

CARE PLAN

ASSESSMENT

SUBJECTIVE DATA:

OBJECTIVE DATA:

NURSING DIAGNOSIS

PROBLEM(S):

ETIOLOGY:

SIGNS AND SYMPTOMS:

PLANNING

GOAL:

DESIRED (MEASURABLE) OUTCOME:

IMPLEMENTATION

INTERVENTIONS:

EVALUATION

OUTCOME:

EVIDENCED BY:

NOTES

SBAR (PATIENT OVERVIEW)

SITUATION

ROOM NAME AGE/SEX CODE ADMIT DATE	DIAGNOSIS MD/CONSULTS ALLERGIES

BACKGROUND

MEDICAL HISTORY	FALL RISK PRECAUTIONS ISOLATION DIET IV & SITE

ASSESSMENT

VITALS	NEURO	RESP
	CARDIO	GI
	GU	MUSCULOSKELETAL
Na Glucose K WBC Mg Hgb Ca Hct Ph Plt Cr PT/INR BUN Other	SKIN	PSYCH

RECOMMENDATIONS

PLAN OF CARE	TO-DO LIST	PATIENT EDUCATION

MEDICATION LIST

GENERIC NAME: **BRAND NAME:**
DOSE: ROUTE: DRUG CLASS:
INDICATION(S): NOTES:

GENERIC NAME: **BRAND NAME:**
DOSE: ROUTE: DRUG CLASS:
INDICATION(S): NOTES:

GENERIC NAME: **BRAND NAME:**
DOSE: ROUTE: DRUG CLASS:
INDICATION(S): NOTES:

GENERIC NAME: **BRAND NAME:**
DOSE: ROUTE: DRUG CLASS:
INDICATION(S): NOTES:

GENERIC NAME: **BRAND NAME:**
DOSE: ROUTE: DRUG CLASS:
INDICATION(S): NOTES:

GENERIC NAME: **BRAND NAME:**
DOSE: ROUTE: DRUG CLASS:
INDICATION(S): NOTES:

GENERIC NAME: **BRAND NAME:**
DOSE: ROUTE: DRUG CLASS:
INDICATION(S): NOTES:

GENERIC NAME: **BRAND NAME:**
DOSE: ROUTE: DRUG CLASS:
INDICATION(S): NOTES:

GENERIC NAME: **BRAND NAME:**
DOSE: ROUTE: DRUG CLASS:
INDICATION(S): NOTES:

GENERIC NAME: **BRAND NAME:**
DOSE: ROUTE: DRUG CLASS:
INDICATION(S): NOTES:

GENERIC NAME: **BRAND NAME:**
DOSE: ROUTE: DRUG CLASS:
INDICATION(S): NOTES:

GENERIC NAME: **BRAND NAME:**
DOSE: ROUTE: DRUG CLASS:
INDICATION(S): NOTES:

CARE PLAN

ASSESSMENT

SUBJECTIVE DATA:

OBJECTIVE DATA:

NURSING DIAGNOSIS

PROBLEM(S):

ETIOLOGY:

SIGNS AND SYMPTOMS:

PLANNING

GOAL:

DESIRED (MEASURABLE) OUTCOME:

IMPLEMENTATION

INTERVENTIONS:

EVALUATION

OUTCOME:

EVIDENCED BY:

NOTES

SBAR (PATIENT OVERVIEW)

SITUATION

ROOM

NAME

AGE/SEX

CODE

ADMIT DATE

DIAGNOSIS

MD/CONSULTS

ALLERGIES

BACKGROUND

MEDICAL HISTORY

FALL RISK

PRECAUTIONS

ISOLATION

DIET

IV & SITE

ASSESSMENT

VITALS

Na	Glucose
K	WBC
Mg	Hgb
Ca	Hct
Ph	Plt
Cr	PT/INR
BUN	Other

NEURO

RESP

CARDIO

GI

GU

MUSCULOSKELETAL

SKIN

PSYCH

RECOMMENDATIONS

PLAN OF CARE

TO-DO LIST

PATIENT EDUCATION

MEDICATION LIST

GENERIC NAME: **BRAND NAME:**
DOSE: ROUTE: DRUG CLASS:
INDICATION(S): NOTES:

GENERIC NAME: **BRAND NAME:**
DOSE: ROUTE: DRUG CLASS:
INDICATION(S): NOTES:

GENERIC NAME: **BRAND NAME:**
DOSE: ROUTE: DRUG CLASS:
INDICATION(S): NOTES:

GENERIC NAME: **BRAND NAME:**
DOSE: ROUTE: DRUG CLASS:
INDICATION(S): NOTES:

GENERIC NAME: **BRAND NAME:**
DOSE: ROUTE: DRUG CLASS:
INDICATION(S): NOTES:

GENERIC NAME: **BRAND NAME:**
DOSE: ROUTE: DRUG CLASS:
INDICATION(S): NOTES:

GENERIC NAME: **BRAND NAME:**
DOSE: ROUTE: DRUG CLASS:
INDICATION(S): NOTES:

GENERIC NAME: **BRAND NAME:**
DOSE: ROUTE: DRUG CLASS:
INDICATION(S): NOTES:

GENERIC NAME: **BRAND NAME:**
DOSE: ROUTE: DRUG CLASS:
INDICATION(S): NOTES:

GENERIC NAME: **BRAND NAME:**
DOSE: ROUTE: DRUG CLASS:
INDICATION(S): NOTES:

GENERIC NAME: **BRAND NAME:**
DOSE: ROUTE: DRUG CLASS:
INDICATION(S): NOTES:

GENERIC NAME: **BRAND NAME:**
DOSE: ROUTE: DRUG CLASS:
INDICATION(S): NOTES:

CARE PLAN

ASSESSMENT

SUBJECTIVE DATA:

OBJECTIVE DATA:

NURSING DIAGNOSIS

PROBLEM(S):

ETIOLOGY:

SIGNS AND SYMPTOMS:

PLANNING

GOAL:

DESIRED (MEASURABLE) OUTCOME:

IMPLEMENTATION

INTERVENTIONS:

EVALUATION

OUTCOME:

EVIDENCED BY:

NOTES

SBAR (PATIENT OVERVIEW)

SITUATION	
ROOM NAME AGE/SEX CODE ADMIT DATE	DIAGNOSIS MD/CONSULTS ALLERGIES

BACKGROUND	
MEDICAL HISTORY	FALL RISK PRECAUTIONS ISOLATION DIET IV & SITE

ASSESSMENT		
VITALS	NEURO	RESP
	CARDIO	GI
	GU	MUSCULOSKELETAL
Na Glucose K WBC Mg Hgb Ca Hct Ph Plt Cr PT/INR BUN Other	SKIN	PSYCH

RECOMMENDATIONS		
PLAN OF CARE	TO-DO LIST	PATIENT EDUCATION

MEDICATION LIST

GENERIC NAME: **BRAND NAME:**
DOSE: ROUTE: DRUG CLASS:
INDICATION(S): NOTES:

GENERIC NAME: **BRAND NAME:**
DOSE: ROUTE: DRUG CLASS:
INDICATION(S): NOTES:

GENERIC NAME: **BRAND NAME:**
DOSE: ROUTE: DRUG CLASS:
INDICATION(S): NOTES:

GENERIC NAME: **BRAND NAME:**
DOSE: ROUTE: DRUG CLASS:
INDICATION(S): NOTES:

GENERIC NAME: **BRAND NAME:**
DOSE: ROUTE: DRUG CLASS:
INDICATION(S): NOTES:

GENERIC NAME: **BRAND NAME:**
DOSE: ROUTE: DRUG CLASS:
INDICATION(S): NOTES:

GENERIC NAME: **BRAND NAME:**
DOSE: ROUTE: DRUG CLASS:
INDICATION(S): NOTES:

GENERIC NAME: **BRAND NAME:**
DOSE: ROUTE: DRUG CLASS:
INDICATION(S): NOTES:

GENERIC NAME: **BRAND NAME:**
DOSE: ROUTE: DRUG CLASS:
INDICATION(S): NOTES:

GENERIC NAME: **BRAND NAME:**
DOSE: ROUTE: DRUG CLASS:
INDICATION(S): NOTES:

GENERIC NAME: **BRAND NAME:**
DOSE: ROUTE: DRUG CLASS:
INDICATION(S): NOTES:

GENERIC NAME: **BRAND NAME:**
DOSE: ROUTE: DRUG CLASS:
INDICATION(S): NOTES:

CARE PLAN

ASSESSMENT

SUBJECTIVE DATA:

OBJECTIVE DATA:

NURSING DIAGNOSIS

PROBLEM(S):

ETIOLOGY:

SIGNS AND SYMPTOMS:

PLANNING

GOAL:

DESIRED (MEASURABLE) OUTCOME:

IMPLEMENTATION

INTERVENTIONS:

EVALUATION

OUTCOME:

EVIDENCED BY:

NOTES

SBAR (PATIENT OVERVIEW)

SITUATION

ROOM NAME AGE/SEX CODE ADMIT DATE	DIAGNOSIS MD/CONSULTS ALLERGIES

BACKGROUND

MEDICAL HISTORY	FALL RISK PRECAUTIONS ISOLATION DIET IV & SITE

ASSESSMENT

VITALS	NEURO	RESP
	CARDIO	GI
	GU	MUSCULOSKELETAL
Na Glucose K WBC Mg Hgb Ca Hct Ph Plt Cr PT/INR BUN Other	SKIN	PSYCH

RECOMMENDATIONS

PLAN OF CARE	TO-DO LIST	PATIENT EDUCATION

MEDICATION LIST

GENERIC NAME: **BRAND NAME:**
DOSE: ROUTE: DRUG CLASS:
INDICATION(S): NOTES:

GENERIC NAME: **BRAND NAME:**
DOSE: ROUTE: DRUG CLASS:
INDICATION(S): NOTES:

GENERIC NAME: **BRAND NAME:**
DOSE: ROUTE: DRUG CLASS:
INDICATION(S): NOTES:

GENERIC NAME: **BRAND NAME:**
DOSE: ROUTE: DRUG CLASS:
INDICATION(S): NOTES:

GENERIC NAME: **BRAND NAME:**
DOSE: ROUTE: DRUG CLASS:
INDICATION(S): NOTES:

GENERIC NAME: **BRAND NAME:**
DOSE: ROUTE: DRUG CLASS:
INDICATION(S): NOTES:

GENERIC NAME: **BRAND NAME:**
DOSE: ROUTE: DRUG CLASS:
INDICATION(S): NOTES:

GENERIC NAME: **BRAND NAME:**
DOSE: ROUTE: DRUG CLASS:
INDICATION(S): NOTES:

GENERIC NAME: **BRAND NAME:**
DOSE: ROUTE: DRUG CLASS:
INDICATION(S): NOTES:

GENERIC NAME: **BRAND NAME:**
DOSE: ROUTE: DRUG CLASS:
INDICATION(S): NOTES:

GENERIC NAME: **BRAND NAME:**
DOSE: ROUTE: DRUG CLASS:
INDICATION(S): NOTES:

GENERIC NAME: **BRAND NAME:**
DOSE: ROUTE: DRUG CLASS:
INDICATION(S): NOTES:

CARE PLAN

ASSESSMENT

SUBJECTIVE DATA:

OBJECTIVE DATA:

NURSING DIAGNOSIS

PROBLEM(S):

ETIOLOGY:

SIGNS AND SYMPTOMS:

PLANNING

GOAL:

DESIRED (MEASURABLE) OUTCOME:

IMPLEMENTATION

INTERVENTIONS:

EVALUATION

OUTCOME:

EVIDENCED BY:

NOTES

SBAR (PATIENT OVERVIEW)

SITUATION

ROOM NAME AGE/SEX CODE ADMIT DATE	DIAGNOSIS MD/CONSULTS ALLERGIES

BACKGROUND

MEDICAL HISTORY	FALL RISK PRECAUTIONS ISOLATION DIET IV & SITE

ASSESSMENT

VITALS	NEURO	RESP
	CARDIO	GI
	GU	MUSCULOSKELETAL
Na Glucose K WBC Mg Hgb Ca Hct Ph Plt Cr PT/INR BUN Other	SKIN	PSYCH

RECOMMENDATIONS

PLAN OF CARE	TO-DO LIST	PATIENT EDUCATION

MEDICATION LIST

GENERIC NAME:		BRAND NAME:
DOSE:	ROUTE:	DRUG CLASS:
INDICATION(S):	NOTES:	
GENERIC NAME:		BRAND NAME:
DOSE:	ROUTE:	DRUG CLASS:
INDICATION(S):	NOTES:	
GENERIC NAME:		BRAND NAME:
DOSE:	ROUTE:	DRUG CLASS:
INDICATION(S):	NOTES:	
GENERIC NAME:		BRAND NAME:
DOSE:	ROUTE:	DRUG CLASS:
INDICATION(S):	NOTES:	
GENERIC NAME:		BRAND NAME:
DOSE:	ROUTE:	DRUG CLASS:
INDICATION(S):	NOTES:	
GENERIC NAME:		BRAND NAME:
DOSE:	ROUTE:	DRUG CLASS:
INDICATION(S):	NOTES:	
GENERIC NAME:		BRAND NAME:
DOSE:	ROUTE:	DRUG CLASS:
INDICATION(S):	NOTES:	
GENERIC NAME:		BRAND NAME:
DOSE:	ROUTE:	DRUG CLASS:
INDICATION(S):	NOTES:	
GENERIC NAME:		BRAND NAME:
DOSE:	ROUTE:	DRUG CLASS:
INDICATION(S):	NOTES:	
GENERIC NAME:		BRAND NAME:
DOSE:	ROUTE:	DRUG CLASS:
INDICATION(S):	NOTES:	
GENERIC NAME:		BRAND NAME:
DOSE:	ROUTE:	DRUG CLASS:
INDICATION(S):	NOTES:	
GENERIC NAME:		BRAND NAME:
DOSE:	ROUTE:	DRUG CLASS:
INDICATION(S):	NOTES:	

CARE PLAN

ASSESSMENT

SUBJECTIVE DATA:

OBJECTIVE DATA:

NURSING DIAGNOSIS

PROBLEM(S):

ETIOLOGY:

SIGNS AND SYMPTOMS:

PLANNING

GOAL:

DESIRED (MEASURABLE) OUTCOME:

IMPLEMENTATION

INTERVENTIONS:

EVALUATION

OUTCOME:

EVIDENCED BY:

NOTES

SBAR (PATIENT OVERVIEW)

SITUATION

ROOM NAME AGE/SEX CODE ADMIT DATE	DIAGNOSIS MD/CONSULTS ALLERGIES

BACKGROUND

MEDICAL HISTORY	FALL RISK PRECAUTIONS ISOLATION DIET IV & SITE

ASSESSMENT

VITALS	NEURO	RESP
	CARDIO	GI
	GU	MUSCULOSKELETAL
Na Glucose K WBC Mg Hgb Ca Hct Ph Plt Cr PT/INR BUN Other	SKIN	PSYCH

RECOMMENDATIONS

PLAN OF CARE	TO-DO LIST	PATIENT EDUCATION

MEDICATION LIST

GENERIC NAME:		**BRAND NAME:**
DOSE:	ROUTE:	DRUG CLASS:
INDICATION(S):	NOTES:	
GENERIC NAME:		**BRAND NAME:**
DOSE:	ROUTE:	DRUG CLASS:
INDICATION(S):	NOTES:	
GENERIC NAME:		**BRAND NAME:**
DOSE:	ROUTE:	DRUG CLASS:
INDICATION(S):	NOTES:	
GENERIC NAME:		**BRAND NAME:**
DOSE:	ROUTE:	DRUG CLASS:
INDICATION(S):	NOTES:	
GENERIC NAME:		**BRAND NAME:**
DOSE:	ROUTE:	DRUG CLASS:
INDICATION(S):	NOTES:	
GENERIC NAME:		**BRAND NAME:**
DOSE:	ROUTE:	DRUG CLASS:
INDICATION(S):	NOTES:	
GENERIC NAME:		**BRAND NAME:**
DOSE:	ROUTE:	DRUG CLASS:
INDICATION(S):	NOTES:	
GENERIC NAME:		**BRAND NAME:**
DOSE:	ROUTE:	DRUG CLASS:
INDICATION(S):	NOTES:	
GENERIC NAME:		**BRAND NAME:**
DOSE:	ROUTE:	DRUG CLASS:
INDICATION(S):	NOTES:	
GENERIC NAME:		**BRAND NAME:**
DOSE:	ROUTE:	DRUG CLASS:
INDICATION(S):	NOTES:	
GENERIC NAME:		**BRAND NAME:**
DOSE:	ROUTE:	DRUG CLASS:
INDICATION(S):	NOTES:	
GENERIC NAME:		**BRAND NAME:**
DOSE:	ROUTE:	DRUG CLASS:
INDICATION(S):	NOTES:	

CARE PLAN

ASSESSMENT

SUBJECTIVE DATA:

OBJECTIVE DATA:

NURSING DIAGNOSIS

PROBLEM(S):

ETIOLOGY:

SIGNS AND SYMPTOMS:

PLANNING

GOAL:

DESIRED (MEASURABLE) OUTCOME:

IMPLEMENTATION

INTERVENTIONS:

EVALUATION

OUTCOME:

EVIDENCED BY:

NOTES

SBAR (PATIENT OVERVIEW)

SITUATION

ROOM NAME AGE/SEX CODE ADMIT DATE	DIAGNOSIS MD/CONSULTS ALLERGIES

BACKGROUND

MEDICAL HISTORY	FALL RISK PRECAUTIONS ISOLATION DIET IV & SITE

ASSESSMENT

VITALS	NEURO	RESP
	CARDIO	GI
Na Glucose K WBC Mg Hgb Ca Hct Ph Plt Cr PT/INR BUN Other	GU	MUSCULOSKELETAL
	SKIN	PSYCH

RECOMMENDATIONS

PLAN OF CARE	TO-DO LIST	PATIENT EDUCATION

MEDICATION LIST

GENERIC NAME: **BRAND NAME:**
DOSE: ROUTE: DRUG CLASS:
INDICATION(S): NOTES:

GENERIC NAME: **BRAND NAME:**
DOSE: ROUTE: DRUG CLASS:
INDICATION(S): NOTES:

GENERIC NAME: **BRAND NAME:**
DOSE: ROUTE: DRUG CLASS:
INDICATION(S): NOTES:

GENERIC NAME: **BRAND NAME:**
DOSE: ROUTE: DRUG CLASS:
INDICATION(S): NOTES:

GENERIC NAME: **BRAND NAME:**
DOSE: ROUTE: DRUG CLASS:
INDICATION(S): NOTES:

GENERIC NAME: **BRAND NAME:**
DOSE: ROUTE: DRUG CLASS:
INDICATION(S): NOTES:

GENERIC NAME: **BRAND NAME:**
DOSE: ROUTE: DRUG CLASS:
INDICATION(S): NOTES:

GENERIC NAME: **BRAND NAME:**
DOSE: ROUTE: DRUG CLASS:
INDICATION(S): NOTES:

GENERIC NAME: **BRAND NAME:**
DOSE: ROUTE: DRUG CLASS:
INDICATION(S): NOTES:

GENERIC NAME: **BRAND NAME:**
DOSE: ROUTE: DRUG CLASS:
INDICATION(S): NOTES:

GENERIC NAME: **BRAND NAME:**
DOSE: ROUTE: DRUG CLASS:
INDICATION(S): NOTES:

GENERIC NAME: **BRAND NAME:**
DOSE: ROUTE: DRUG CLASS:
INDICATION(S): NOTES:

CARE PLAN

ASSESSMENT

SUBJECTIVE DATA:

OBJECTIVE DATA:

NURSING DIAGNOSIS

PROBLEM(S):

ETIOLOGY:

SIGNS AND SYMPTOMS:

PLANNING

GOAL:

DESIRED (MEASURABLE) OUTCOME:

IMPLEMENTATION

INTERVENTIONS:

EVALUATION

OUTCOME:

EVIDENCED BY:

NOTES

SBAR (PATIENT OVERVIEW)

SITUATION

ROOM NAME AGE/SEX CODE ADMIT DATE	DIAGNOSIS
	MD/CONSULTS
	ALLERGIES

BACKGROUND

MEDICAL HISTORY	FALL RISK PRECAUTIONS ISOLATION DIET IV & SITE

ASSESSMENT

VITALS	NEURO	RESP
	CARDIO	GI
	GU	MUSCULOSKELETAL
Na Glucose K WBC Mg Hgb Ca Hct Ph Plt Cr PT/INR BUN Other	SKIN	PSYCH

RECOMMENDATIONS

PLAN OF CARE	TO-DO LIST	PATIENT EDUCATION

MEDICATION LIST

GENERIC NAME: **BRAND NAME:**
DOSE: ROUTE: DRUG CLASS:
INDICATION(S): NOTES:

GENERIC NAME: **BRAND NAME:**
DOSE: ROUTE: DRUG CLASS:
INDICATION(S): NOTES:

GENERIC NAME: **BRAND NAME:**
DOSE: ROUTE: DRUG CLASS:
INDICATION(S): NOTES:

GENERIC NAME: **BRAND NAME:**
DOSE: ROUTE: DRUG CLASS:
INDICATION(S): NOTES:

GENERIC NAME: **BRAND NAME:**
DOSE: ROUTE: DRUG CLASS:
INDICATION(S): NOTES:

GENERIC NAME: **BRAND NAME:**
DOSE: ROUTE: DRUG CLASS:
INDICATION(S): NOTES:

GENERIC NAME: **BRAND NAME:**
DOSE: ROUTE: DRUG CLASS:
INDICATION(S): NOTES:

GENERIC NAME: **BRAND NAME:**
DOSE: ROUTE: DRUG CLASS:
INDICATION(S): NOTES:

GENERIC NAME: **BRAND NAME:**
DOSE: ROUTE: DRUG CLASS:
INDICATION(S): NOTES:

GENERIC NAME: **BRAND NAME:**
DOSE: ROUTE: DRUG CLASS:
INDICATION(S): NOTES:

GENERIC NAME: **BRAND NAME:**
DOSE: ROUTE: DRUG CLASS:
INDICATION(S): NOTES:

GENERIC NAME: **BRAND NAME:**
DOSE: ROUTE: DRUG CLASS:
INDICATION(S): NOTES:

CARE PLAN

ASSESSMENT

SUBJECTIVE DATA:

OBJECTIVE DATA:

NURSING DIAGNOSIS

PROBLEM(S):

ETIOLOGY:

SIGNS AND SYMPTOMS:

PLANNING

GOAL:

DESIRED (MEASURABLE) OUTCOME:

IMPLEMENTATION

INTERVENTIONS:

EVALUATION

OUTCOME:

EVIDENCED BY:

NOTES

SBAR (PATIENT OVERVIEW)

SITUATION

ROOM NAME AGE/SEX CODE ADMIT DATE	DIAGNOSIS MD/CONSULTS ALLERGIES

BACKGROUND

MEDICAL HISTORY	FALL RISK PRECAUTIONS ISOLATION DIET IV & SITE

ASSESSMENT

VITALS	NEURO	RESP
	CARDIO	GI
	GU	MUSCULOSKELETAL
Na Glucose K WBC Mg Hgb Ca Hct Ph Plt Cr PT/INR BUN Other	SKIN	PSYCH

RECOMMENDATIONS

PLAN OF CARE	TO-DO LIST	PATIENT EDUCATION

MEDICATION LIST

GENERIC NAME:		**BRAND NAME:**
DOSE:	ROUTE:	DRUG CLASS:
INDICATION(S):	NOTES:	

GENERIC NAME:		**BRAND NAME:**
DOSE:	ROUTE:	DRUG CLASS:
INDICATION(S):	NOTES:	

GENERIC NAME:		**BRAND NAME:**
DOSE:	ROUTE:	DRUG CLASS:
INDICATION(S):	NOTES:	

GENERIC NAME:		**BRAND NAME:**
DOSE:	ROUTE:	DRUG CLASS:
INDICATION(S):	NOTES:	

GENERIC NAME:		**BRAND NAME:**
DOSE:	ROUTE:	DRUG CLASS:
INDICATION(S):	NOTES:	

GENERIC NAME:		**BRAND NAME:**
DOSE:	ROUTE:	DRUG CLASS:
INDICATION(S):	NOTES:	

GENERIC NAME:		**BRAND NAME:**
DOSE:	ROUTE:	DRUG CLASS:
INDICATION(S):	NOTES:	

GENERIC NAME:		**BRAND NAME:**
DOSE:	ROUTE:	DRUG CLASS:
INDICATION(S):	NOTES:	

GENERIC NAME:		**BRAND NAME:**
DOSE:	ROUTE:	DRUG CLASS:
INDICATION(S):	NOTES:	

GENERIC NAME:		**BRAND NAME:**
DOSE:	ROUTE:	DRUG CLASS:
INDICATION(S):	NOTES:	

GENERIC NAME:		**BRAND NAME:**
DOSE:	ROUTE:	DRUG CLASS:
INDICATION(S):	NOTES:	

GENERIC NAME:		**BRAND NAME:**
DOSE:	ROUTE:	DRUG CLASS:
INDICATION(S):	NOTES:	

CARE PLAN

ASSESSMENT

SUBJECTIVE DATA:

OBJECTIVE DATA:

NURSING DIAGNOSIS

PROBLEM(S):

ETIOLOGY:

SIGNS AND SYMPTOMS:

PLANNING

GOAL:

DESIRED (MEASURABLE) OUTCOME:

IMPLEMENTATION

INTERVENTIONS:

EVALUATION

OUTCOME:

EVIDENCED BY:

NOTES

SBAR (PATIENT OVERVIEW)

SITUATION	
ROOM NAME AGE/SEX CODE ADMIT DATE	DIAGNOSIS MD/CONSULTS ALLERGIES

BACKGROUND	
MEDICAL HISTORY	FALL RISK PRECAUTIONS ISOLATION DIET IV & SITE

ASSESSMENT		
VITALS	NEURO	RESP
	CARDIO	GI
	GU	MUSCULOSKELETAL
Na Glucose K WBC Mg Hgb Ca Hct Ph Plt Cr PT/INR BUN Other	SKIN	PSYCH

RECOMMENDATIONS		
PLAN OF CARE	TO-DO LIST	PATIENT EDUCATION

MEDICATION LIST

GENERIC NAME:		BRAND NAME:
DOSE:	ROUTE:	DRUG CLASS:
INDICATION(S):	NOTES:	

GENERIC NAME:		BRAND NAME:
DOSE:	ROUTE:	DRUG CLASS:
INDICATION(S):	NOTES:	

GENERIC NAME:		BRAND NAME:
DOSE:	ROUTE:	DRUG CLASS:
INDICATION(S):	NOTES:	

GENERIC NAME:		BRAND NAME:
DOSE:	ROUTE:	DRUG CLASS:
INDICATION(S):	NOTES:	

GENERIC NAME:		BRAND NAME:
DOSE:	ROUTE:	DRUG CLASS:
INDICATION(S):	NOTES:	

GENERIC NAME:		BRAND NAME:
DOSE:	ROUTE:	DRUG CLASS:
INDICATION(S):	NOTES:	

GENERIC NAME:		BRAND NAME:
DOSE:	ROUTE:	DRUG CLASS:
INDICATION(S):	NOTES:	

GENERIC NAME:		BRAND NAME:
DOSE:	ROUTE:	DRUG CLASS:
INDICATION(S):	NOTES:	

GENERIC NAME:		BRAND NAME:
DOSE:	ROUTE:	DRUG CLASS:
INDICATION(S):	NOTES:	

GENERIC NAME:		BRAND NAME:
DOSE:	ROUTE:	DRUG CLASS:
INDICATION(S):	NOTES:	

GENERIC NAME:		BRAND NAME:
DOSE:	ROUTE:	DRUG CLASS:
INDICATION(S):	NOTES:	

GENERIC NAME:		BRAND NAME:
DOSE:	ROUTE:	DRUG CLASS:
INDICATION(S):	NOTES:	

CARE PLAN

ASSESSMENT

SUBJECTIVE DATA:

OBJECTIVE DATA:

NURSING DIAGNOSIS

PROBLEM(S):

ETIOLOGY:

SIGNS AND SYMPTOMS:

PLANNING

GOAL:

DESIRED (MEASURABLE) OUTCOME:

IMPLEMENTATION

INTERVENTIONS:

EVALUATION

OUTCOME:

EVIDENCED BY:

NOTES

SBAR (PATIENT OVERVIEW)

SITUATION

ROOM NAME AGE/SEX CODE ADMIT DATE	DIAGNOSIS MD/CONSULTS ALLERGIES

BACKGROUND

MEDICAL HISTORY	FALL RISK PRECAUTIONS ISOLATION DIET IV & SITE

ASSESSMENT

VITALS	NEURO	RESP
	CARDIO	GI
	GU	MUSCULOSKELETAL
Na / Glucose K / WBC Mg / Hgb Ca / Hct Ph / Plt Cr / PT/INR BUN / Other	SKIN	PSYCH

RECOMMENDATIONS

PLAN OF CARE	TO-DO LIST	PATIENT EDUCATION

MEDICATION LIST

GENERIC NAME: **BRAND NAME:**
DOSE: ROUTE: DRUG CLASS:
INDICATION(S): NOTES:

GENERIC NAME: **BRAND NAME:**
DOSE: ROUTE: DRUG CLASS:
INDICATION(S): NOTES:

GENERIC NAME: **BRAND NAME:**
DOSE: ROUTE: DRUG CLASS:
INDICATION(S): NOTES:

GENERIC NAME: **BRAND NAME:**
DOSE: ROUTE: DRUG CLASS:
INDICATION(S): NOTES:

GENERIC NAME: **BRAND NAME:**
DOSE: ROUTE: DRUG CLASS:
INDICATION(S): NOTES:

GENERIC NAME: **BRAND NAME:**
DOSE: ROUTE: DRUG CLASS:
INDICATION(S): NOTES:

GENERIC NAME: **BRAND NAME:**
DOSE: ROUTE: DRUG CLASS:
INDICATION(S): NOTES:

GENERIC NAME: **BRAND NAME:**
DOSE: ROUTE: DRUG CLASS:
INDICATION(S): NOTES:

GENERIC NAME: **BRAND NAME:**
DOSE: ROUTE: DRUG CLASS:
INDICATION(S): NOTES:

GENERIC NAME: **BRAND NAME:**
DOSE: ROUTE: DRUG CLASS:
INDICATION(S): NOTES:

GENERIC NAME: **BRAND NAME:**
DOSE: ROUTE: DRUG CLASS:
INDICATION(S): NOTES:

GENERIC NAME: **BRAND NAME:**
DOSE: ROUTE: DRUG CLASS:
INDICATION(S): NOTES:

CARE PLAN

ASSESSMENT

SUBJECTIVE DATA:

OBJECTIVE DATA:

NURSING DIAGNOSIS

PROBLEM(S):

ETIOLOGY:

SIGNS AND SYMPTOMS:

PLANNING

GOAL:

DESIRED (MEASURABLE) OUTCOME:

IMPLEMENTATION

INTERVENTIONS:

EVALUATION

OUTCOME:

EVIDENCED BY:

NOTES

SBAR (PATIENT OVERVIEW)

SITUATION

ROOM

NAME

AGE/SEX

CODE

ADMIT DATE

DIAGNOSIS

MD/CONSULTS

ALLERGIES

BACKGROUND

MEDICAL HISTORY

FALL RISK

PRECAUTIONS

ISOLATION

DIET

IV & SITE

ASSESSMENT

VITALS

Na	Glucose
K	WBC
Mg	Hgb
Ca	Hct
Ph	Plt
Cr	PT/INR
BUN	Other

NEURO

RESP

CARDIO

GI

GU

MUSCULOSKELETAL

SKIN

PSYCH

RECOMMENDATIONS

PLAN OF CARE

TO-DO LIST

PATIENT EDUCATION

MEDICATION LIST

GENERIC NAME: BRAND NAME:
DOSE: ROUTE: DRUG CLASS:
INDICATION(S): NOTES:

GENERIC NAME: BRAND NAME:
DOSE: ROUTE: DRUG CLASS:
INDICATION(S): NOTES:

GENERIC NAME: BRAND NAME:
DOSE: ROUTE: DRUG CLASS:
INDICATION(S): NOTES:

GENERIC NAME: BRAND NAME:
DOSE: ROUTE: DRUG CLASS:
INDICATION(S): NOTES:

GENERIC NAME: BRAND NAME:
DOSE: ROUTE: DRUG CLASS:
INDICATION(S): NOTES:

GENERIC NAME: BRAND NAME:
DOSE: ROUTE: DRUG CLASS:
INDICATION(S): NOTES:

GENERIC NAME: BRAND NAME:
DOSE: ROUTE: DRUG CLASS:
INDICATION(S): NOTES:

GENERIC NAME: BRAND NAME:
DOSE: ROUTE: DRUG CLASS:
INDICATION(S): NOTES:

GENERIC NAME: BRAND NAME:
DOSE: ROUTE: DRUG CLASS:
INDICATION(S): NOTES:

GENERIC NAME: BRAND NAME:
DOSE: ROUTE: DRUG CLASS:
INDICATION(S): NOTES:

GENERIC NAME: BRAND NAME:
DOSE: ROUTE: DRUG CLASS:
INDICATION(S): NOTES:

GENERIC NAME: BRAND NAME:
DOSE: ROUTE: DRUG CLASS:
INDICATION(S): NOTES:

CARE PLAN

ASSESSMENT

SUBJECTIVE DATA:

OBJECTIVE DATA:

NURSING DIAGNOSIS

PROBLEM(S):

ETIOLOGY:

SIGNS AND SYMPTOMS:

PLANNING

GOAL:

DESIRED (MEASURABLE) OUTCOME:

IMPLEMENTATION

INTERVENTIONS:

EVALUATION

OUTCOME:

EVIDENCED BY:

NOTES

SBAR (PATIENT OVERVIEW)

SITUATION

ROOM NAME AGE/SEX CODE ADMIT DATE	DIAGNOSIS MD/CONSULTS ALLERGIES

BACKGROUND

MEDICAL HISTORY	FALL RISK PRECAUTIONS ISOLATION DIET IV & SITE

ASSESSMENT

VITALS	NEURO	RESP
	CARDIO	GI
	GU	MUSCULOSKELETAL
Na / Glucose K / WBC Mg / Hgb Ca / Hct Ph / Plt Cr / PT/INR BUN / Other	SKIN	PSYCH

RECOMMENDATIONS

PLAN OF CARE	TO-DO LIST	PATIENT EDUCATION

MEDICATION LIST

GENERIC NAME: **BRAND NAME:**
DOSE: ROUTE: DRUG CLASS:
INDICATION(S): NOTES:

GENERIC NAME: **BRAND NAME:**
DOSE: ROUTE: DRUG CLASS:
INDICATION(S): NOTES:

GENERIC NAME: **BRAND NAME:**
DOSE: ROUTE: DRUG CLASS:
INDICATION(S): NOTES:

GENERIC NAME: **BRAND NAME:**
DOSE: ROUTE: DRUG CLASS:
INDICATION(S): NOTES:

GENERIC NAME: **BRAND NAME:**
DOSE: ROUTE: DRUG CLASS:
INDICATION(S): NOTES:

GENERIC NAME: **BRAND NAME:**
DOSE: ROUTE: DRUG CLASS:
INDICATION(S): NOTES:

GENERIC NAME: **BRAND NAME:**
DOSE: ROUTE: DRUG CLASS:
INDICATION(S): NOTES:

GENERIC NAME: **BRAND NAME:**
DOSE: ROUTE: DRUG CLASS:
INDICATION(S): NOTES:

GENERIC NAME: **BRAND NAME:**
DOSE: ROUTE: DRUG CLASS:
INDICATION(S): NOTES:

GENERIC NAME: **BRAND NAME:**
DOSE: ROUTE: DRUG CLASS:
INDICATION(S): NOTES:

GENERIC NAME: **BRAND NAME:**
DOSE: ROUTE: DRUG CLASS:
INDICATION(S): NOTES:

GENERIC NAME: **BRAND NAME:**
DOSE: ROUTE: DRUG CLASS:
INDICATION(S): NOTES:

CARE PLAN

ASSESSMENT

SUBJECTIVE DATA:

OBJECTIVE DATA:

NURSING DIAGNOSIS

PROBLEM(S):

ETIOLOGY:

SIGNS AND SYMPTOMS:

PLANNING

GOAL:

DESIRED (MEASURABLE) OUTCOME:

IMPLEMENTATION

INTERVENTIONS:

EVALUATION

OUTCOME:

EVIDENCED BY:

NOTES

SBAR (PATIENT OVERVIEW)

SITUATION

ROOM NAME AGE/SEX CODE ADMIT DATE	DIAGNOSIS MD/CONSULTS ALLERGIES

BACKGROUND

MEDICAL HISTORY	FALL RISK PRECAUTIONS ISOLATION DIET IV & SITE

ASSESSMENT

VITALS	NEURO	RESP
	CARDIO	GI
	GU	MUSCULOSKELETAL
Na Glucose K WBC Mg Hgb Ca Hct Ph Plt Cr PT/INR BUN Other	SKIN	PSYCH

RECOMMENDATIONS

PLAN OF CARE	TO-DO LIST	PATIENT EDUCATION

MEDICATION LIST

GENERIC NAME: **BRAND NAME:**
DOSE: ROUTE: DRUG CLASS:
INDICATION(S): NOTES:

GENERIC NAME: **BRAND NAME:**
DOSE: ROUTE: DRUG CLASS:
INDICATION(S): NOTES:

GENERIC NAME: **BRAND NAME:**
DOSE: ROUTE: DRUG CLASS:
INDICATION(S): NOTES:

GENERIC NAME: **BRAND NAME:**
DOSE: ROUTE: DRUG CLASS:
INDICATION(S): NOTES:

GENERIC NAME: **BRAND NAME:**
DOSE: ROUTE: DRUG CLASS:
INDICATION(S): NOTES:

GENERIC NAME: **BRAND NAME:**
DOSE: ROUTE: DRUG CLASS:
INDICATION(S): NOTES:

GENERIC NAME: **BRAND NAME:**
DOSE: ROUTE: DRUG CLASS:
INDICATION(S): NOTES:

GENERIC NAME: **BRAND NAME:**
DOSE: ROUTE: DRUG CLASS:
INDICATION(S): NOTES:

GENERIC NAME: **BRAND NAME:**
DOSE: ROUTE: DRUG CLASS:
INDICATION(S): NOTES:

GENERIC NAME: **BRAND NAME:**
DOSE: ROUTE: DRUG CLASS:
INDICATION(S): NOTES:

GENERIC NAME: **BRAND NAME:**
DOSE: ROUTE: DRUG CLASS:
INDICATION(S): NOTES:

GENERIC NAME: **BRAND NAME:**
DOSE: ROUTE: DRUG CLASS:
INDICATION(S): NOTES:

CARE PLAN

ASSESSMENT

SUBJECTIVE DATA:

OBJECTIVE DATA:

NURSING DIAGNOSIS

PROBLEM(S):

ETIOLOGY:

SIGNS AND SYMPTOMS:

PLANNING

GOAL:

DESIRED (MEASURABLE) OUTCOME:

IMPLEMENTATION

INTERVENTIONS:

EVALUATION

OUTCOME:

EVIDENCED BY:

NOTES

SBAR (PATIENT OVERVIEW)

SITUATION	
ROOM NAME AGE/SEX CODE ADMIT DATE	DIAGNOSIS MD/CONSULTS ALLERGIES

BACKGROUND	
MEDICAL HISTORY	FALL RISK PRECAUTIONS ISOLATION DIET IV & SITE

ASSESSMENT			
VITALS		NEURO	RESP
		CARDIO	GI
		GU	MUSCULOSKELETAL
Na K Mg Ca Ph Cr BUN	Glucose WBC Hgb Hct Plt PT/INR Other	SKIN	PSYCH

RECOMMENDATIONS		
PLAN OF CARE	TO-DO LIST	PATIENT EDUCATION

MEDICATION LIST

GENERIC NAME: **BRAND NAME:**
DOSE: ROUTE: DRUG CLASS:
INDICATION(S): NOTES:

GENERIC NAME: **BRAND NAME:**
DOSE: ROUTE: DRUG CLASS:
INDICATION(S): NOTES:

GENERIC NAME: **BRAND NAME:**
DOSE: ROUTE: DRUG CLASS:
INDICATION(S): NOTES:

GENERIC NAME: **BRAND NAME:**
DOSE: ROUTE: DRUG CLASS:
INDICATION(S): NOTES:

GENERIC NAME: **BRAND NAME:**
DOSE: ROUTE: DRUG CLASS:
INDICATION(S): NOTES:

GENERIC NAME: **BRAND NAME:**
DOSE: ROUTE: DRUG CLASS:
INDICATION(S): NOTES:

GENERIC NAME: **BRAND NAME:**
DOSE: ROUTE: DRUG CLASS:
INDICATION(S): NOTES:

GENERIC NAME: **BRAND NAME:**
DOSE: ROUTE: DRUG CLASS:
INDICATION(S): NOTES:

GENERIC NAME: **BRAND NAME:**
DOSE: ROUTE: DRUG CLASS:
INDICATION(S): NOTES:

GENERIC NAME: **BRAND NAME:**
DOSE: ROUTE: DRUG CLASS:
INDICATION(S): NOTES:

GENERIC NAME: **BRAND NAME:**
DOSE: ROUTE: DRUG CLASS:
INDICATION(S): NOTES:

GENERIC NAME: **BRAND NAME:**
DOSE: ROUTE: DRUG CLASS:
INDICATION(S): NOTES:

CARE PLAN

ASSESSMENT

SUBJECTIVE DATA:

OBJECTIVE DATA:

NURSING DIAGNOSIS

PROBLEM(S):

ETIOLOGY:

SIGNS AND SYMPTOMS:

PLANNING

GOAL:

DESIRED (MEASURABLE) OUTCOME:

IMPLEMENTATION

INTERVENTIONS:

EVALUATION

OUTCOME:

EVIDENCED BY:

NOTES

SBAR (PATIENT OVERVIEW)

SITUATION

ROOM

NAME

AGE/SEX

CODE

ADMIT DATE

DIAGNOSIS

MD/CONSULTS

ALLERGIES

BACKGROUND

MEDICAL HISTORY

FALL RISK

PRECAUTIONS

ISOLATION

DIET

IV & SITE

ASSESSMENT

VITALS

Na	Glucose
K	WBC
Mg	Hgb
Ca	Hct
Ph	Plt
Cr	PT/INR
BUN	Other

NEURO

RESP

CARDIO

GI

GU

MUSCULOSKELETAL

SKIN

PSYCH

RECOMMENDATIONS

PLAN OF CARE

TO-DO LIST

PATIENT EDUCATION

MEDICATION LIST

GENERIC NAME:		BRAND NAME:
DOSE:	ROUTE:	DRUG CLASS:
INDICATION(S):	NOTES:	
GENERIC NAME:		BRAND NAME:
DOSE:	ROUTE:	DRUG CLASS:
INDICATION(S):	NOTES:	
GENERIC NAME:		BRAND NAME:
DOSE:	ROUTE:	DRUG CLASS:
INDICATION(S):	NOTES:	
GENERIC NAME:		BRAND NAME:
DOSE:	ROUTE:	DRUG CLASS:
INDICATION(S):	NOTES:	
GENERIC NAME:		BRAND NAME:
DOSE:	ROUTE:	DRUG CLASS:
INDICATION(S):	NOTES:	
GENERIC NAME:		BRAND NAME:
DOSE:	ROUTE:	DRUG CLASS:
INDICATION(S):	NOTES:	
GENERIC NAME:		BRAND NAME:
DOSE:	ROUTE:	DRUG CLASS:
INDICATION(S):	NOTES:	
GENERIC NAME:		BRAND NAME:
DOSE:	ROUTE:	DRUG CLASS:
INDICATION(S):	NOTES:	
GENERIC NAME:		BRAND NAME:
DOSE:	ROUTE:	DRUG CLASS:
INDICATION(S):	NOTES:	
GENERIC NAME:		BRAND NAME:
DOSE:	ROUTE:	DRUG CLASS:
INDICATION(S):	NOTES:	
GENERIC NAME:		BRAND NAME:
DOSE:	ROUTE:	DRUG CLASS:
INDICATION(S):	NOTES:	
GENERIC NAME:		BRAND NAME:
DOSE:	ROUTE:	DRUG CLASS:
INDICATION(S):	NOTES:	

CARE PLAN

ASSESSMENT

SUBJECTIVE DATA:

OBJECTIVE DATA:

NURSING DIAGNOSIS

PROBLEM(S):

ETIOLOGY:

SIGNS AND SYMPTOMS:

PLANNING

GOAL:

DESIRED (MEASURABLE) OUTCOME:

IMPLEMENTATION

INTERVENTIONS:

EVALUATION

OUTCOME:

EVIDENCED BY:

NOTES

SBAR (PATIENT OVERVIEW)

SITUATION

ROOM NAME AGE/SEX CODE ADMIT DATE	DIAGNOSIS MD/CONSULTS ALLERGIES

BACKGROUND

MEDICAL HISTORY	FALL RISK PRECAUTIONS ISOLATION DIET IV & SITE

ASSESSMENT

VITALS	NEURO	RESP
	CARDIO	GI
Na Glucose K WBC Mg Hgb Ca Hct Ph Plt Cr PT/INR BUN Other	GU	MUSCULOSKELETAL
	SKIN	PSYCH

RECOMMENDATIONS

PLAN OF CARE	TO-DO LIST	PATIENT EDUCATION

MEDICATION LIST

GENERIC NAME:		BRAND NAME:
DOSE:	ROUTE:	DRUG CLASS:
INDICATION(S):	NOTES:	
GENERIC NAME:		BRAND NAME:
DOSE:	ROUTE:	DRUG CLASS:
INDICATION(S):	NOTES:	
GENERIC NAME:		BRAND NAME:
DOSE:	ROUTE:	DRUG CLASS:
INDICATION(S):	NOTES:	
GENERIC NAME:		BRAND NAME:
DOSE:	ROUTE:	DRUG CLASS:
INDICATION(S):	NOTES:	
GENERIC NAME:		BRAND NAME:
DOSE:	ROUTE:	DRUG CLASS:
INDICATION(S):	NOTES:	
GENERIC NAME:		BRAND NAME:
DOSE:	ROUTE:	DRUG CLASS:
INDICATION(S):	NOTES:	
GENERIC NAME:		BRAND NAME:
DOSE:	ROUTE:	DRUG CLASS:
INDICATION(S):	NOTES:	
GENERIC NAME:		BRAND NAME:
DOSE:	ROUTE:	DRUG CLASS:
INDICATION(S):	NOTES:	
GENERIC NAME:		BRAND NAME:
DOSE:	ROUTE:	DRUG CLASS:
INDICATION(S):	NOTES:	
GENERIC NAME:		BRAND NAME:
DOSE:	ROUTE:	DRUG CLASS:
INDICATION(S):	NOTES:	
GENERIC NAME:		BRAND NAME:
DOSE:	ROUTE:	DRUG CLASS:
INDICATION(S):	NOTES:	
GENERIC NAME:		BRAND NAME:
DOSE:	ROUTE:	DRUG CLASS:
INDICATION(S):	NOTES:	

CARE PLAN

ASSESSMENT

SUBJECTIVE DATA:

OBJECTIVE DATA:

NURSING DIAGNOSIS

PROBLEM(S):

ETIOLOGY:

SIGNS AND SYMPTOMS:

PLANNING

GOAL:

DESIRED (MEASURABLE) OUTCOME:

IMPLEMENTATION

INTERVENTIONS:

EVALUATION

OUTCOME:

EVIDENCED BY:

NOTES

SBAR (PATIENT OVERVIEW)

SITUATION

ROOM NAME AGE/SEX CODE ADMIT DATE	DIAGNOSIS MD/CONSULTS ALLERGIES

BACKGROUND

MEDICAL HISTORY	FALL RISK PRECAUTIONS ISOLATION DIET IV & SITE

ASSESSMENT

VITALS	NEURO	RESP
	CARDIO	GI
	GU	MUSCULOSKELETAL
Na Glucose K WBC Mg Hgb Ca Hct Ph Plt Cr PT/INR BUN Other	SKIN	PSYCH

RECOMMENDATIONS

PLAN OF CARE	TO-DO LIST	PATIENT EDUCATION

MEDICATION LIST

GENERIC NAME: BRAND NAME:
DOSE: ROUTE: DRUG CLASS:
INDICATION(S): NOTES:

GENERIC NAME: BRAND NAME:
DOSE: ROUTE: DRUG CLASS:
INDICATION(S): NOTES:

GENERIC NAME: BRAND NAME:
DOSE: ROUTE: DRUG CLASS:
INDICATION(S): NOTES:

GENERIC NAME: BRAND NAME:
DOSE: ROUTE: DRUG CLASS:
INDICATION(S): NOTES:

GENERIC NAME: BRAND NAME:
DOSE: ROUTE: DRUG CLASS:
INDICATION(S): NOTES:

GENERIC NAME: BRAND NAME:
DOSE: ROUTE: DRUG CLASS:
INDICATION(S): NOTES:

GENERIC NAME: BRAND NAME:
DOSE: ROUTE: DRUG CLASS:
INDICATION(S): NOTES:

GENERIC NAME: BRAND NAME:
DOSE: ROUTE: DRUG CLASS:
INDICATION(S): NOTES:

GENERIC NAME: BRAND NAME:
DOSE: ROUTE: DRUG CLASS:
INDICATION(S): NOTES:

GENERIC NAME: BRAND NAME:
DOSE: ROUTE: DRUG CLASS:
INDICATION(S): NOTES:

GENERIC NAME: BRAND NAME:
DOSE: ROUTE: DRUG CLASS:
INDICATION(S): NOTES:

GENERIC NAME: BRAND NAME:
DOSE: ROUTE: DRUG CLASS:
INDICATION(S): NOTES:

CARE PLAN

ASSESSMENT

SUBJECTIVE DATA:

OBJECTIVE DATA:

NURSING DIAGNOSIS

PROBLEM(S):

ETIOLOGY:

SIGNS AND SYMPTOMS:

PLANNING

GOAL:

DESIRED (MEASURABLE) OUTCOME:

IMPLEMENTATION

INTERVENTIONS:

EVALUATION

OUTCOME:

EVIDENCED BY:

NOTES

SBAR (PATIENT OVERVIEW)

SITUATION

ROOM NAME AGE/SEX CODE ADMIT DATE	DIAGNOSIS MD/CONSULTS ALLERGIES

BACKGROUND

MEDICAL HISTORY	FALL RISK PRECAUTIONS ISOLATION DIET IV & SITE

ASSESSMENT

VITALS	NEURO	RESP
	CARDIO	GI
Na / Glucose K / WBC Mg / Hgb Ca / Hct Ph / Plt Cr / PT/INR BUN / Other	GU	MUSCULOSKELETAL
	SKIN	PSYCH

RECOMMENDATIONS

PLAN OF CARE	TO-DO LIST	PATIENT EDUCATION

MEDICATION LIST

GENERIC NAME: **BRAND NAME:**
DOSE: ROUTE: DRUG CLASS:
INDICATION(S): NOTES:

GENERIC NAME: **BRAND NAME:**
DOSE: ROUTE: DRUG CLASS:
INDICATION(S): NOTES:

GENERIC NAME: **BRAND NAME:**
DOSE: ROUTE: DRUG CLASS:
INDICATION(S): NOTES:

GENERIC NAME: **BRAND NAME:**
DOSE: ROUTE: DRUG CLASS:
INDICATION(S): NOTES:

GENERIC NAME: **BRAND NAME:**
DOSE: ROUTE: DRUG CLASS:
INDICATION(S): NOTES:

GENERIC NAME: **BRAND NAME:**
DOSE: ROUTE: DRUG CLASS:
INDICATION(S): NOTES:

GENERIC NAME: **BRAND NAME:**
DOSE: ROUTE: DRUG CLASS:
INDICATION(S): NOTES:

GENERIC NAME: **BRAND NAME:**
DOSE: ROUTE: DRUG CLASS:
INDICATION(S): NOTES:

GENERIC NAME: **BRAND NAME:**
DOSE: ROUTE: DRUG CLASS:
INDICATION(S): NOTES:

GENERIC NAME: **BRAND NAME:**
DOSE: ROUTE: DRUG CLASS:
INDICATION(S): NOTES:

GENERIC NAME: **BRAND NAME:**
DOSE: ROUTE: DRUG CLASS:
INDICATION(S): NOTES:

GENERIC NAME: **BRAND NAME:**
DOSE: ROUTE: DRUG CLASS:
INDICATION(S): NOTES:

CARE PLAN

ASSESSMENT

SUBJECTIVE DATA:

OBJECTIVE DATA:

NURSING DIAGNOSIS

PROBLEM(S):

ETIOLOGY:

SIGNS AND SYMPTOMS:

PLANNING

GOAL:

DESIRED (MEASURABLE) OUTCOME:

IMPLEMENTATION

INTERVENTIONS:

EVALUATION

OUTCOME:

EVIDENCED BY:

NOTES

SBAR (PATIENT OVERVIEW)

SITUATION

ROOM NAME AGE/SEX CODE ADMIT DATE	DIAGNOSIS MD/CONSULTS ALLERGIES

BACKGROUND

MEDICAL HISTORY	FALL RISK PRECAUTIONS ISOLATION DIET IV & SITE

ASSESSMENT

VITALS	NEURO	RESP
	CARDIO	GI
	GU	MUSCULOSKELETAL
Na Glucose K WBC Mg Hgb Ca Hct Ph Plt Cr PT/INR BUN Other	SKIN	PSYCH

RECOMMENDATIONS

PLAN OF CARE	TO-DO LIST	PATIENT EDUCATION

MEDICATION LIST

GENERIC NAME: **BRAND NAME:**
DOSE: ROUTE: DRUG CLASS:
INDICATION(S): NOTES:

GENERIC NAME: **BRAND NAME:**
DOSE: ROUTE: DRUG CLASS:
INDICATION(S): NOTES:

GENERIC NAME: **BRAND NAME:**
DOSE: ROUTE: DRUG CLASS:
INDICATION(S): NOTES:

GENERIC NAME: **BRAND NAME:**
DOSE: ROUTE: DRUG CLASS:
INDICATION(S): NOTES:

GENERIC NAME: **BRAND NAME:**
DOSE: ROUTE: DRUG CLASS:
INDICATION(S): NOTES:

GENERIC NAME: **BRAND NAME:**
DOSE: ROUTE: DRUG CLASS:
INDICATION(S): NOTES:

GENERIC NAME: **BRAND NAME:**
DOSE: ROUTE: DRUG CLASS:
INDICATION(S): NOTES:

GENERIC NAME: **BRAND NAME:**
DOSE: ROUTE: DRUG CLASS:
INDICATION(S): NOTES:

GENERIC NAME: **BRAND NAME:**
DOSE: ROUTE: DRUG CLASS:
INDICATION(S): NOTES:

GENERIC NAME: **BRAND NAME:**
DOSE: ROUTE: DRUG CLASS:
INDICATION(S): NOTES:

GENERIC NAME: **BRAND NAME:**
DOSE: ROUTE: DRUG CLASS:
INDICATION(S): NOTES:

GENERIC NAME: **BRAND NAME:**
DOSE: ROUTE: DRUG CLASS:
INDICATION(S): NOTES:

CARE PLAN

ASSESSMENT

SUBJECTIVE DATA:

OBJECTIVE DATA:

NURSING DIAGNOSIS

PROBLEM(S):

ETIOLOGY:

SIGNS AND SYMPTOMS:

PLANNING

GOAL:

DESIRED (MEASURABLE) OUTCOME:

IMPLEMENTATION

INTERVENTIONS:

EVALUATION

OUTCOME:

EVIDENCED BY:

NOTES

SBAR (PATIENT OVERVIEW)

SITUATION

ROOM NAME AGE/SEX CODE ADMIT DATE	DIAGNOSIS MD/CONSULTS ALLERGIES

BACKGROUND

MEDICAL HISTORY	FALL RISK PRECAUTIONS ISOLATION DIET IV & SITE

ASSESSMENT

VITALS	NEURO	RESP
	CARDIO	GI
	GU	MUSCULOSKELETAL
Na Glucose K WBC Mg Hgb Ca Hct Ph Plt Cr PT/INR BUN Other	SKIN	PSYCH

RECOMMENDATIONS

PLAN OF CARE	TO-DO LIST	PATIENT EDUCATION

MEDICATION LIST

GENERIC NAME: **BRAND NAME:**
DOSE: ROUTE: DRUG CLASS:
INDICATION(S): NOTES:

GENERIC NAME: **BRAND NAME:**
DOSE: ROUTE: DRUG CLASS:
INDICATION(S): NOTES:

GENERIC NAME: **BRAND NAME:**
DOSE: ROUTE: DRUG CLASS:
INDICATION(S): NOTES:

GENERIC NAME: **BRAND NAME:**
DOSE: ROUTE: DRUG CLASS:
INDICATION(S): NOTES:

GENERIC NAME: **BRAND NAME:**
DOSE: ROUTE: DRUG CLASS:
INDICATION(S): NOTES:

GENERIC NAME: **BRAND NAME:**
DOSE: ROUTE: DRUG CLASS:
INDICATION(S): NOTES:

GENERIC NAME: **BRAND NAME:**
DOSE: ROUTE: DRUG CLASS:
INDICATION(S): NOTES:

GENERIC NAME: **BRAND NAME:**
DOSE: ROUTE: DRUG CLASS:
INDICATION(S): NOTES:

GENERIC NAME: **BRAND NAME:**
DOSE: ROUTE: DRUG CLASS:
INDICATION(S): NOTES:

GENERIC NAME: **BRAND NAME:**
DOSE: ROUTE: DRUG CLASS:
INDICATION(S): NOTES:

GENERIC NAME: **BRAND NAME:**
DOSE: ROUTE: DRUG CLASS:
INDICATION(S): NOTES:

GENERIC NAME: **BRAND NAME:**
DOSE: ROUTE: DRUG CLASS:
INDICATION(S): NOTES:

CARE PLAN

ASSESSMENT

SUBJECTIVE DATA:

OBJECTIVE DATA:

NURSING DIAGNOSIS

PROBLEM(S):

ETIOLOGY:

SIGNS AND SYMPTOMS:

PLANNING

GOAL:

DESIRED (MEASURABLE) OUTCOME:

IMPLEMENTATION

INTERVENTIONS:

EVALUATION

OUTCOME:

EVIDENCED BY:

NOTES

SBAR (PATIENT OVERVIEW)

SITUATION	
ROOM NAME AGE/SEX CODE ADMIT DATE	DIAGNOSIS MD/CONSULTS ALLERGIES

BACKGROUND	
MEDICAL HISTORY	FALL RISK PRECAUTIONS ISOLATION DIET IV & SITE

ASSESSMENT			
VITALS		NEURO	RESP
		CARDIO	GI
		GU	MUSCULOSKELETAL
Na	Glucose		
K	WBC		
Mg	Hgb	SKIN	PSYCH
Ca	Hct		
Ph	Plt		
Cr	PT/INR		
BUN	Other		

RECOMMENDATIONS		
PLAN OF CARE	TO-DO LIST	PATIENT EDUCATION

MEDICATION LIST

GENERIC NAME: **BRAND NAME:**
DOSE: ROUTE: DRUG CLASS:
INDICATION(S): NOTES:

GENERIC NAME: **BRAND NAME:**
DOSE: ROUTE: DRUG CLASS:
INDICATION(S): NOTES:

GENERIC NAME: **BRAND NAME:**
DOSE: ROUTE: DRUG CLASS:
INDICATION(S): NOTES:

GENERIC NAME: **BRAND NAME:**
DOSE: ROUTE: DRUG CLASS:
INDICATION(S): NOTES:

GENERIC NAME: **BRAND NAME:**
DOSE: ROUTE: DRUG CLASS:
INDICATION(S): NOTES:

GENERIC NAME: **BRAND NAME:**
DOSE: ROUTE: DRUG CLASS:
INDICATION(S): NOTES:

GENERIC NAME: **BRAND NAME:**
DOSE: ROUTE: DRUG CLASS:
INDICATION(S): NOTES:

GENERIC NAME: **BRAND NAME:**
DOSE: ROUTE: DRUG CLASS:
INDICATION(S): NOTES:

GENERIC NAME: **BRAND NAME:**
DOSE: ROUTE: DRUG CLASS:
INDICATION(S): NOTES:

GENERIC NAME: **BRAND NAME:**
DOSE: ROUTE: DRUG CLASS:
INDICATION(S): NOTES:

GENERIC NAME: **BRAND NAME:**
DOSE: ROUTE: DRUG CLASS:
INDICATION(S): NOTES:

GENERIC NAME: **BRAND NAME:**
DOSE: ROUTE: DRUG CLASS:
INDICATION(S): NOTES:

GENERIC NAME: **BRAND NAME:**
DOSE: ROUTE: DRUG CLASS:
INDICATION(S): NOTES:

CARE PLAN

ASSESSMENT

SUBJECTIVE DATA:

OBJECTIVE DATA:

NURSING DIAGNOSIS

PROBLEM(S):

ETIOLOGY:

SIGNS AND SYMPTOMS:

PLANNING

GOAL:

DESIRED (MEASURABLE) OUTCOME:

IMPLEMENTATION

INTERVENTIONS:

EVALUATION

OUTCOME:

EVIDENCED BY:

NOTES

SBAR (PATIENT OVERVIEW)

SITUATION

ROOM NAME AGE/SEX CODE ADMIT DATE	DIAGNOSIS MD/CONSULTS ALLERGIES

BACKGROUND

MEDICAL HISTORY	FALL RISK PRECAUTIONS ISOLATION DIET IV & SITE

ASSESSMENT

VITALS	NEURO	RESP
	CARDIO	GI
	GU	MUSCULOSKELETAL
Na Glucose K WBC Mg Hgb Ca Hct Ph Plt Cr PT/INR BUN Other	SKIN	PSYCH

RECOMMENDATIONS

PLAN OF CARE	TO-DO LIST	PATIENT EDUCATION

MEDICATION LIST

GENERIC NAME:		**BRAND NAME:**
DOSE:	ROUTE:	DRUG CLASS:
INDICATION(S):	NOTES:	
GENERIC NAME:		**BRAND NAME:**
DOSE:	ROUTE:	DRUG CLASS:
INDICATION(S):	NOTES:	
GENERIC NAME:		**BRAND NAME:**
DOSE:	ROUTE:	DRUG CLASS:
INDICATION(S):	NOTES:	
GENERIC NAME:		**BRAND NAME:**
DOSE:	ROUTE:	DRUG CLASS:
INDICATION(S):	NOTES:	
GENERIC NAME:		**BRAND NAME:**
DOSE:	ROUTE:	DRUG CLASS:
INDICATION(S):	NOTES:	
GENERIC NAME:		**BRAND NAME:**
DOSE:	ROUTE:	DRUG CLASS:
INDICATION(S):	NOTES:	
GENERIC NAME:		**BRAND NAME:**
DOSE:	ROUTE:	DRUG CLASS:
INDICATION(S):	NOTES:	
GENERIC NAME:		**BRAND NAME:**
DOSE:	ROUTE:	DRUG CLASS:
INDICATION(S):	NOTES:	
GENERIC NAME:		**BRAND NAME:**
DOSE:	ROUTE:	DRUG CLASS:
INDICATION(S):	NOTES:	
GENERIC NAME:		**BRAND NAME:**
DOSE:	ROUTE:	DRUG CLASS:
INDICATION(S):	NOTES:	
GENERIC NAME:		**BRAND NAME:**
DOSE:	ROUTE:	DRUG CLASS:
INDICATION(S):	NOTES:	
GENERIC NAME:		**BRAND NAME:**
DOSE:	ROUTE:	DRUG CLASS:
INDICATION(S):	NOTES:	

CARE PLAN

ASSESSMENT

SUBJECTIVE DATA:

OBJECTIVE DATA:

NURSING DIAGNOSIS

PROBLEM(S):

ETIOLOGY:

SIGNS AND SYMPTOMS:

PLANNING

GOAL:

DESIRED (MEASURABLE) OUTCOME:

IMPLEMENTATION

INTERVENTIONS:

EVALUATION

OUTCOME:

EVIDENCED BY:

NOTES

SBAR (PATIENT OVERVIEW)

SITUATION

ROOM NAME AGE/SEX CODE ADMIT DATE	DIAGNOSIS MD/CONSULTS ALLERGIES

BACKGROUND

MEDICAL HISTORY	FALL RISK PRECAUTIONS ISOLATION DIET IV & SITE

ASSESSMENT

VITALS	NEURO	RESP
	CARDIO	GI
	GU	MUSCULOSKELETAL
Na Glucose K WBC Mg Hgb Ca Hct Ph Plt Cr PT/INR BUN Other	SKIN	PSYCH

RECOMMENDATIONS

PLAN OF CARE	TO-DO LIST	PATIENT EDUCATION

MEDICATION LIST

GENERIC NAME: **BRAND NAME:**
DOSE: ROUTE: DRUG CLASS:
INDICATION(S): NOTES:

GENERIC NAME: **BRAND NAME:**
DOSE: ROUTE: DRUG CLASS:
INDICATION(S): NOTES:

GENERIC NAME: **BRAND NAME:**
DOSE: ROUTE: DRUG CLASS:
INDICATION(S): NOTES:

GENERIC NAME: **BRAND NAME:**
DOSE: ROUTE: DRUG CLASS:
INDICATION(S): NOTES:

GENERIC NAME: **BRAND NAME:**
DOSE: ROUTE: DRUG CLASS:
INDICATION(S): NOTES:

GENERIC NAME: **BRAND NAME:**
DOSE: ROUTE: DRUG CLASS:
INDICATION(S): NOTES:

GENERIC NAME: **BRAND NAME:**
DOSE: ROUTE: DRUG CLASS:
INDICATION(S): NOTES:

GENERIC NAME: **BRAND NAME:**
DOSE: ROUTE: DRUG CLASS:
INDICATION(S): NOTES:

GENERIC NAME: **BRAND NAME:**
DOSE: ROUTE: DRUG CLASS:
INDICATION(S): NOTES:

GENERIC NAME: **BRAND NAME:**
DOSE: ROUTE: DRUG CLASS:
INDICATION(S): NOTES:

GENERIC NAME: **BRAND NAME:**
DOSE: ROUTE: DRUG CLASS:
INDICATION(S): NOTES:

GENERIC NAME: **BRAND NAME:**
DOSE: ROUTE: DRUG CLASS:
INDICATION(S): NOTES:

CARE PLAN

ASSESSMENT

SUBJECTIVE DATA:

OBJECTIVE DATA:

NURSING DIAGNOSIS

PROBLEM(S):

ETIOLOGY:

SIGNS AND SYMPTOMS:

PLANNING

GOAL:

DESIRED (MEASURABLE) OUTCOME:

IMPLEMENTATION

INTERVENTIONS:

EVALUATION

OUTCOME:

EVIDENCED BY:

NOTES

SBAR (PATIENT OVERVIEW)

SITUATION	
ROOM NAME AGE/SEX CODE ADMIT DATE	DIAGNOSIS MD/CONSULTS ALLERGIES

BACKGROUND	
MEDICAL HISTORY	FALL RISK PRECAUTIONS ISOLATION DIET IV & SITE

ASSESSMENT		
VITALS	NEURO	RESP
	CARDIO	GI
	GU	MUSCULOSKELETAL
Na Glucose K WBC Mg Hgb Ca Hct Ph Plt Cr PT/INR BUN Other	SKIN	PSYCH

RECOMMENDATIONS		
PLAN OF CARE	TO-DO LIST	PATIENT EDUCATION

MEDICATION LIST

GENERIC NAME: **BRAND NAME:**
DOSE: ROUTE: DRUG CLASS:
INDICATION(S): NOTES:

GENERIC NAME: **BRAND NAME:**
DOSE: ROUTE: DRUG CLASS:
INDICATION(S): NOTES:

GENERIC NAME: **BRAND NAME:**
DOSE: ROUTE: DRUG CLASS:
INDICATION(S): NOTES:

GENERIC NAME: **BRAND NAME:**
DOSE: ROUTE: DRUG CLASS:
INDICATION(S): NOTES:

GENERIC NAME: **BRAND NAME:**
DOSE: ROUTE: DRUG CLASS:
INDICATION(S): NOTES:

GENERIC NAME: **BRAND NAME:**
DOSE: ROUTE: DRUG CLASS:
INDICATION(S): NOTES:

GENERIC NAME: **BRAND NAME:**
DOSE: ROUTE: DRUG CLASS:
INDICATION(S): NOTES:

GENERIC NAME: **BRAND NAME:**
DOSE: ROUTE: DRUG CLASS:
INDICATION(S): NOTES:

GENERIC NAME: **BRAND NAME:**
DOSE: ROUTE: DRUG CLASS:
INDICATION(S): NOTES:

GENERIC NAME: **BRAND NAME:**
DOSE: ROUTE: DRUG CLASS:
INDICATION(S): NOTES:

GENERIC NAME: **BRAND NAME:**
DOSE: ROUTE: DRUG CLASS:
INDICATION(S): NOTES:

GENERIC NAME: **BRAND NAME:**
DOSE: ROUTE: DRUG CLASS:
INDICATION(S): NOTES:

CARE PLAN

ASSESSMENT

SUBJECTIVE DATA:

OBJECTIVE DATA:

NURSING DIAGNOSIS

PROBLEM(S):

ETIOLOGY:

SIGNS AND SYMPTOMS:

PLANNING

GOAL:

DESIRED (MEASURABLE) OUTCOME:

IMPLEMENTATION

INTERVENTIONS:

EVALUATION

OUTCOME:

EVIDENCED BY:

NOTES

SBAR (PATIENT OVERVIEW)

SITUATION	
ROOM NAME AGE/SEX CODE ADMIT DATE	DIAGNOSIS MD/CONSULTS ALLERGIES

BACKGROUND	
MEDICAL HISTORY	FALL RISK PRECAUTIONS ISOLATION DIET IV & SITE

ASSESSMENT		
VITALS	NEURO	RESP
	CARDIO	GI
	GU	MUSCULOSKELETAL
Na Glucose K WBC Mg Hgb Ca Hct Ph Plt Cr PT/INR BUN Other	SKIN	PSYCH

RECOMMENDATIONS		
PLAN OF CARE	TO-DO LIST	PATIENT EDUCATION

MEDICATION LIST

GENERIC NAME:		BRAND NAME:	
DOSE:	ROUTE:		DRUG CLASS:
INDICATION(S):		NOTES:	
GENERIC NAME:		**BRAND NAME:**	
DOSE:	ROUTE:		DRUG CLASS:
INDICATION(S):		NOTES:	
GENERIC NAME:		**BRAND NAME:**	
DOSE:	ROUTE:		DRUG CLASS:
INDICATION(S):		NOTES:	
GENERIC NAME:		**BRAND NAME:**	
DOSE:	ROUTE:		DRUG CLASS:
INDICATION(S):		NOTES:	
GENERIC NAME:		**BRAND NAME:**	
DOSE:	ROUTE:		DRUG CLASS:
INDICATION(S):		NOTES:	
GENERIC NAME:		**BRAND NAME:**	
DOSE:	ROUTE:		DRUG CLASS:
INDICATION(S):		NOTES:	
GENERIC NAME:		**BRAND NAME:**	
DOSE:	ROUTE:		DRUG CLASS:
INDICATION(S):		NOTES:	
GENERIC NAME:		**BRAND NAME:**	
DOSE:	ROUTE:		DRUG CLASS:
INDICATION(S):		NOTES:	
GENERIC NAME:		**BRAND NAME:**	
DOSE:	ROUTE:		DRUG CLASS:
INDICATION(S):		NOTES:	
GENERIC NAME:		**BRAND NAME:**	
DOSE:	ROUTE:		DRUG CLASS:
INDICATION(S):		NOTES:	
GENERIC NAME:		**BRAND NAME:**	
DOSE:	ROUTE:		DRUG CLASS:
INDICATION(S):		NOTES:	
GENERIC NAME:		**BRAND NAME:**	
DOSE:	ROUTE:		DRUG CLASS:
INDICATION(S):		NOTES:	

CARE PLAN

ASSESSMENT

SUBJECTIVE DATA:

OBJECTIVE DATA:

NURSING DIAGNOSIS

PROBLEM(S):

ETIOLOGY:

SIGNS AND SYMPTOMS:

PLANNING

GOAL:

DESIRED (MEASURABLE) OUTCOME:

IMPLEMENTATION

INTERVENTIONS:

EVALUATION

OUTCOME:

EVIDENCED BY:

NOTES

SBAR (PATIENT OVERVIEW)

SITUATION

ROOM NAME AGE/SEX CODE ADMIT DATE	DIAGNOSIS MD/CONSULTS ALLERGIES

BACKGROUND

MEDICAL HISTORY	FALL RISK PRECAUTIONS ISOLATION DIET IV & SITE

ASSESSMENT

VITALS	NEURO	RESP
	CARDIO	GI
	GU	MUSCULOSKELETAL
Na Glucose K WBC Mg Hgb Ca Hct Ph Plt Cr PT/INR BUN Other	SKIN	PSYCH

RECOMMENDATIONS

PLAN OF CARE	TO-DO LIST	PATIENT EDUCATION

MEDICATION LIST

GENERIC NAME: **BRAND NAME:**
DOSE: ROUTE: DRUG CLASS:
INDICATION(S): NOTES:

GENERIC NAME: **BRAND NAME:**
DOSE: ROUTE: DRUG CLASS:
INDICATION(S): NOTES:

GENERIC NAME: **BRAND NAME:**
DOSE: ROUTE: DRUG CLASS:
INDICATION(S): NOTES:

GENERIC NAME: **BRAND NAME:**
DOSE: ROUTE: DRUG CLASS:
INDICATION(S): NOTES:

GENERIC NAME: **BRAND NAME:**
DOSE: ROUTE: DRUG CLASS:
INDICATION(S): NOTES:

GENERIC NAME: **BRAND NAME:**
DOSE: ROUTE: DRUG CLASS:
INDICATION(S): NOTES:

GENERIC NAME: **BRAND NAME:**
DOSE: ROUTE: DRUG CLASS:
INDICATION(S): NOTES:

GENERIC NAME: **BRAND NAME:**
DOSE: ROUTE: DRUG CLASS:
INDICATION(S): NOTES:

GENERIC NAME: **BRAND NAME:**
DOSE: ROUTE: DRUG CLASS:
INDICATION(S): NOTES:

GENERIC NAME: **BRAND NAME:**
DOSE: ROUTE: DRUG CLASS:
INDICATION(S): NOTES:

GENERIC NAME: **BRAND NAME:**
DOSE: ROUTE: DRUG CLASS:
INDICATION(S): NOTES:

GENERIC NAME: **BRAND NAME:**
DOSE: ROUTE: DRUG CLASS:
INDICATION(S): NOTES:

CARE PLAN

ASSESSMENT

SUBJECTIVE DATA:

OBJECTIVE DATA:

NURSING DIAGNOSIS

PROBLEM(S):

ETIOLOGY:

SIGNS AND SYMPTOMS:

PLANNING

GOAL:

DESIRED (MEASURABLE) OUTCOME:

IMPLEMENTATION

INTERVENTIONS:

EVALUATION

OUTCOME:

EVIDENCED BY:

NOTES

SBAR (PATIENT OVERVIEW)

SITUATION	
ROOM NAME AGE/SEX CODE ADMIT DATE	DIAGNOSIS MD/CONSULTS ALLERGIES

BACKGROUND	
MEDICAL HISTORY	FALL RISK PRECAUTIONS ISOLATION DIET IV & SITE

ASSESSMENT			
VITALS		NEURO	RESP
		CARDIO	GI
		GU	MUSCULOSKELETAL
Na K Mg Ca Ph Cr BUN	Glucose WBC Hgb Hct Plt PT/INR Other	SKIN	PSYCH

RECOMMENDATIONS		
PLAN OF CARE	TO-DO LIST	PATIENT EDUCATION

MEDICATION LIST

GENERIC NAME: **BRAND NAME:**
DOSE: ROUTE: DRUG CLASS:
INDICATION(S): NOTES:

GENERIC NAME: **BRAND NAME:**
DOSE: ROUTE: DRUG CLASS:
INDICATION(S): NOTES:

GENERIC NAME: **BRAND NAME:**
DOSE: ROUTE: DRUG CLASS:
INDICATION(S): NOTES:

GENERIC NAME: **BRAND NAME:**
DOSE: ROUTE: DRUG CLASS:
INDICATION(S): NOTES:

GENERIC NAME: **BRAND NAME:**
DOSE: ROUTE: DRUG CLASS:
INDICATION(S): NOTES:

GENERIC NAME: **BRAND NAME:**
DOSE: ROUTE: DRUG CLASS:
INDICATION(S): NOTES:

GENERIC NAME: **BRAND NAME:**
DOSE: ROUTE: DRUG CLASS:
INDICATION(S): NOTES:

GENERIC NAME: **BRAND NAME:**
DOSE: ROUTE: DRUG CLASS:
INDICATION(S): NOTES:

GENERIC NAME: **BRAND NAME:**
DOSE: ROUTE: DRUG CLASS:
INDICATION(S): NOTES:

GENERIC NAME: **BRAND NAME:**
DOSE: ROUTE: DRUG CLASS:
INDICATION(S): NOTES:

GENERIC NAME: **BRAND NAME:**
DOSE: ROUTE: DRUG CLASS:
INDICATION(S): NOTES:

GENERIC NAME: **BRAND NAME:**
DOSE: ROUTE: DRUG CLASS:
INDICATION(S): NOTES:

CARE PLAN

ASSESSMENT

SUBJECTIVE DATA:

OBJECTIVE DATA:

NURSING DIAGNOSIS

PROBLEM(S):

ETIOLOGY:

SIGNS AND SYMPTOMS:

PLANNING

GOAL:

DESIRED (MEASURABLE) OUTCOME:

IMPLEMENTATION

INTERVENTIONS:

EVALUATION

OUTCOME:

EVIDENCED BY:

NOTES

SBAR (PATIENT OVERVIEW)

SITUATION

ROOM NAME AGE/SEX CODE ADMIT DATE	DIAGNOSIS MD/CONSULTS ALLERGIES

BACKGROUND

MEDICAL HISTORY	FALL RISK PRECAUTIONS ISOLATION DIET IV & SITE

ASSESSMENT

VITALS	NEURO	RESP
	CARDIO	GI
	GU	MUSCULOSKELETAL
Na Glucose K WBC Mg Hgb Ca Hct Ph Plt Cr PT/INR BUN Other	SKIN	PSYCH

RECOMMENDATIONS

PLAN OF CARE	TO-DO LIST	PATIENT EDUCATION

MEDICATION LIST

GENERIC NAME: **BRAND NAME:**
DOSE: ROUTE: DRUG CLASS:
INDICATION(S): NOTES:

GENERIC NAME: **BRAND NAME:**
DOSE: ROUTE: DRUG CLASS:
INDICATION(S): NOTES:

GENERIC NAME: **BRAND NAME:**
DOSE: ROUTE: DRUG CLASS:
INDICATION(S): NOTES:

GENERIC NAME: **BRAND NAME:**
DOSE: ROUTE: DRUG CLASS:
INDICATION(S): NOTES:

GENERIC NAME: **BRAND NAME:**
DOSE: ROUTE: DRUG CLASS:
INDICATION(S): NOTES:

GENERIC NAME: **BRAND NAME:**
DOSE: ROUTE: DRUG CLASS:
INDICATION(S): NOTES:

GENERIC NAME: **BRAND NAME:**
DOSE: ROUTE: DRUG CLASS:
INDICATION(S): NOTES:

GENERIC NAME: **BRAND NAME:**
DOSE: ROUTE: DRUG CLASS:
INDICATION(S): NOTES:

GENERIC NAME: **BRAND NAME:**
DOSE: ROUTE: DRUG CLASS:
INDICATION(S): NOTES:

GENERIC NAME: **BRAND NAME:**
DOSE: ROUTE: DRUG CLASS:
INDICATION(S): NOTES:

GENERIC NAME: **BRAND NAME:**
DOSE: ROUTE: DRUG CLASS:
INDICATION(S): NOTES:

GENERIC NAME: **BRAND NAME:**
DOSE: ROUTE: DRUG CLASS:
INDICATION(S): NOTES:

CARE PLAN

ASSESSMENT

SUBJECTIVE DATA:

OBJECTIVE DATA:

NURSING DIAGNOSIS

PROBLEM(S):

ETIOLOGY:

SIGNS AND SYMPTOMS:

PLANNING

GOAL:

DESIRED (MEASURABLE) OUTCOME:

IMPLEMENTATION

INTERVENTIONS:

EVALUATION

OUTCOME:

EVIDENCED BY:

NOTES

SBAR (PATIENT OVERVIEW)

SITUATION

ROOM NAME AGE/SEX CODE ADMIT DATE	DIAGNOSIS MD/CONSULTS ALLERGIES

BACKGROUND

MEDICAL HISTORY	FALL RISK PRECAUTIONS ISOLATION DIET IV & SITE

ASSESSMENT

VITALS	NEURO	RESP
	CARDIO	GI
	GU	MUSCULOSKELETAL
Na / Glucose K / WBC Mg / Hgb Ca / Hct Ph / Plt Cr / PT/INR BUN / Other	SKIN	PSYCH

RECOMMENDATIONS

PLAN OF CARE	TO-DO LIST	PATIENT EDUCATION

MEDICATION LIST

GENERIC NAME: **BRAND NAME:**
DOSE: ROUTE: DRUG CLASS:
INDICATION(S): NOTES:

GENERIC NAME: **BRAND NAME:**
DOSE: ROUTE: DRUG CLASS:
INDICATION(S): NOTES:

GENERIC NAME: **BRAND NAME:**
DOSE: ROUTE: DRUG CLASS:
INDICATION(S): NOTES:

GENERIC NAME: **BRAND NAME:**
DOSE: ROUTE: DRUG CLASS:
INDICATION(S): NOTES:

GENERIC NAME: **BRAND NAME:**
DOSE: ROUTE: DRUG CLASS:
INDICATION(S): NOTES:

GENERIC NAME: **BRAND NAME:**
DOSE: ROUTE: DRUG CLASS:
INDICATION(S): NOTES:

GENERIC NAME: **BRAND NAME:**
DOSE: ROUTE: DRUG CLASS:
INDICATION(S): NOTES:

GENERIC NAME: **BRAND NAME:**
DOSE: ROUTE: DRUG CLASS:
INDICATION(S): NOTES:

GENERIC NAME: **BRAND NAME:**
DOSE: ROUTE: DRUG CLASS:
INDICATION(S): NOTES:

GENERIC NAME: **BRAND NAME:**
DOSE: ROUTE: DRUG CLASS:
INDICATION(S): NOTES:

GENERIC NAME: **BRAND NAME:**
DOSE: ROUTE: DRUG CLASS:
INDICATION(S): NOTES:

GENERIC NAME: **BRAND NAME:**
DOSE: ROUTE: DRUG CLASS:
INDICATION(S): NOTES:

CARE PLAN

ASSESSMENT

SUBJECTIVE DATA:

OBJECTIVE DATA:

NURSING DIAGNOSIS

PROBLEM(S):

ETIOLOGY:

SIGNS AND SYMPTOMS:

PLANNING

GOAL:

DESIRED (MEASURABLE) OUTCOME:

IMPLEMENTATION

INTERVENTIONS:

EVALUATION

OUTCOME:

EVIDENCED BY:

NOTES

SBAR (PATIENT OVERVIEW)

SITUATION

ROOM NAME AGE/SEX CODE ADMIT DATE	DIAGNOSIS MD/CONSULTS ALLERGIES

BACKGROUND

MEDICAL HISTORY	FALL RISK PRECAUTIONS ISOLATION DIET IV & SITE

ASSESSMENT

VITALS	NEURO	RESP
	CARDIO	GI
	GU	MUSCULOSKELETAL
Na Glucose K WBC Mg Hgb Ca Hct Ph Plt Cr PT/INR BUN Other	SKIN	PSYCH

RECOMMENDATIONS

PLAN OF CARE	TO-DO LIST	PATIENT EDUCATION

MEDICATION LIST

GENERIC NAME: **BRAND NAME:**
DOSE: ROUTE: DRUG CLASS:
INDICATION(S): NOTES:

GENERIC NAME: **BRAND NAME:**
DOSE: ROUTE: DRUG CLASS:
INDICATION(S): NOTES:

GENERIC NAME: **BRAND NAME:**
DOSE: ROUTE: DRUG CLASS:
INDICATION(S): NOTES:

GENERIC NAME: **BRAND NAME:**
DOSE: ROUTE: DRUG CLASS:
INDICATION(S): NOTES:

GENERIC NAME: **BRAND NAME:**
DOSE: ROUTE: DRUG CLASS:
INDICATION(S): NOTES:

GENERIC NAME: **BRAND NAME:**
DOSE: ROUTE: DRUG CLASS:
INDICATION(S): NOTES:

GENERIC NAME: **BRAND NAME:**
DOSE: ROUTE: DRUG CLASS:
INDICATION(S): NOTES:

GENERIC NAME: **BRAND NAME:**
DOSE: ROUTE: DRUG CLASS:
INDICATION(S): NOTES:

GENERIC NAME: **BRAND NAME:**
DOSE: ROUTE: DRUG CLASS:
INDICATION(S): NOTES:

GENERIC NAME: **BRAND NAME:**
DOSE: ROUTE: DRUG CLASS:
INDICATION(S): NOTES:

GENERIC NAME: **BRAND NAME:**
DOSE: ROUTE: DRUG CLASS:
INDICATION(S): NOTES:

GENERIC NAME: **BRAND NAME:**
DOSE: ROUTE: DRUG CLASS:
INDICATION(S): NOTES:

CARE PLAN

ASSESSMENT

SUBJECTIVE DATA:

OBJECTIVE DATA:

NURSING DIAGNOSIS

PROBLEM(S):

ETIOLOGY:

SIGNS AND SYMPTOMS:

PLANNING

GOAL:

DESIRED (MEASURABLE) OUTCOME:

IMPLEMENTATION

INTERVENTIONS:

EVALUATION

OUTCOME:

EVIDENCED BY:

NOTES

SBAR (PATIENT OVERVIEW)

SITUATION

ROOM NAME AGE/SEX CODE ADMIT DATE	DIAGNOSIS MD/CONSULTS ALLERGIES

BACKGROUND

MEDICAL HISTORY	FALL RISK PRECAUTIONS ISOLATION DIET IV & SITE

ASSESSMENT

VITALS	NEURO	RESP
	CARDIO	GI
	GU	MUSCULOSKELETAL
Na Glucose K WBC Mg Hgb Ca Hct Ph Plt Cr PT/INR BUN Other	SKIN	PSYCH

RECOMMENDATIONS

PLAN OF CARE	TO-DO LIST	PATIENT EDUCATION

MEDICATION LIST

GENERIC NAME:		BRAND NAME:
DOSE:	ROUTE:	DRUG CLASS:
INDICATION(S):	NOTES:	
GENERIC NAME:		**BRAND NAME:**
DOSE:	ROUTE:	DRUG CLASS:
INDICATION(S):	NOTES:	
GENERIC NAME:		**BRAND NAME:**
DOSE:	ROUTE:	DRUG CLASS:
INDICATION(S):	NOTES:	
GENERIC NAME:		**BRAND NAME:**
DOSE:	ROUTE:	DRUG CLASS:
INDICATION(S):	NOTES:	
GENERIC NAME:		**BRAND NAME:**
DOSE:	ROUTE:	DRUG CLASS:
INDICATION(S):	NOTES:	
GENERIC NAME:		**BRAND NAME:**
DOSE:	ROUTE:	DRUG CLASS:
INDICATION(S):	NOTES:	
GENERIC NAME:		**BRAND NAME:**
DOSE:	ROUTE:	DRUG CLASS:
INDICATION(S):	NOTES:	
GENERIC NAME:		**BRAND NAME:**
DOSE:	ROUTE:	DRUG CLASS:
INDICATION(S):	NOTES:	
GENERIC NAME:		**BRAND NAME:**
DOSE:	ROUTE:	DRUG CLASS:
INDICATION(S):	NOTES:	
GENERIC NAME:		**BRAND NAME:**
DOSE:	ROUTE:	DRUG CLASS:
INDICATION(S):	NOTES:	
GENERIC NAME:		**BRAND NAME:**
DOSE:	ROUTE:	DRUG CLASS:
INDICATION(S):	NOTES:	
GENERIC NAME:		**BRAND NAME:**
DOSE:	ROUTE:	DRUG CLASS:
INDICATION(S):	NOTES:	

CARE PLAN

ASSESSMENT

SUBJECTIVE DATA:

OBJECTIVE DATA:

NURSING DIAGNOSIS

PROBLEM(S):

ETIOLOGY:

SIGNS AND SYMPTOMS:

PLANNING

GOAL:

DESIRED (MEASURABLE) OUTCOME:

IMPLEMENTATION

INTERVENTIONS:

EVALUATION

OUTCOME:

EVIDENCED BY:

NOTES

SBAR (PATIENT OVERVIEW)

SITUATION

ROOM NAME AGE/SEX CODE ADMIT DATE	DIAGNOSIS MD/CONSULTS ALLERGIES

BACKGROUND

MEDICAL HISTORY	FALL RISK PRECAUTIONS ISOLATION DIET IV & SITE

ASSESSMENT

VITALS	NEURO	RESP
	CARDIO	GI
	GU	MUSCULOSKELETAL
Na Glucose K WBC Mg Hgb Ca Hct Ph Plt Cr PT/INR BUN Other	SKIN	PSYCH

RECOMMENDATIONS

PLAN OF CARE	TO-DO LIST	PATIENT EDUCATION

MEDICATION LIST

GENERIC NAME: **BRAND NAME:**
DOSE: ROUTE: DRUG CLASS:
INDICATION(S): NOTES:

GENERIC NAME: **BRAND NAME:**
DOSE: ROUTE: DRUG CLASS:
INDICATION(S): NOTES:

GENERIC NAME: **BRAND NAME:**
DOSE: ROUTE: DRUG CLASS:
INDICATION(S): NOTES:

GENERIC NAME: **BRAND NAME:**
DOSE: ROUTE: DRUG CLASS:
INDICATION(S): NOTES:

GENERIC NAME: **BRAND NAME:**
DOSE: ROUTE: DRUG CLASS:
INDICATION(S): NOTES:

GENERIC NAME: **BRAND NAME:**
DOSE: ROUTE: DRUG CLASS:
INDICATION(S): NOTES:

GENERIC NAME: **BRAND NAME:**
DOSE: ROUTE: DRUG CLASS:
INDICATION(S): NOTES:

GENERIC NAME: **BRAND NAME:**
DOSE: ROUTE: DRUG CLASS:
INDICATION(S): NOTES:

GENERIC NAME: **BRAND NAME:**
DOSE: ROUTE: DRUG CLASS:
INDICATION(S): NOTES:

GENERIC NAME: **BRAND NAME:**
DOSE: ROUTE: DRUG CLASS:
INDICATION(S): NOTES:

GENERIC NAME: **BRAND NAME:**
DOSE: ROUTE: DRUG CLASS:
INDICATION(S): NOTES:

GENERIC NAME: **BRAND NAME:**
DOSE: ROUTE: DRUG CLASS:
INDICATION(S): NOTES:

CARE PLAN

ASSESSMENT

SUBJECTIVE DATA:

OBJECTIVE DATA:

NURSING DIAGNOSIS

PROBLEM(S):

ETIOLOGY:

SIGNS AND SYMPTOMS:

PLANNING

GOAL:

DESIRED (MEASURABLE) OUTCOME:

IMPLEMENTATION

INTERVENTIONS:

EVALUATION

OUTCOME:

EVIDENCED BY:

NOTES

SBAR (PATIENT OVERVIEW)

SITUATION

ROOM NAME AGE/SEX CODE ADMIT DATE	DIAGNOSIS MD/CONSULTS ALLERGIES

BACKGROUND

MEDICAL HISTORY	FALL RISK PRECAUTIONS ISOLATION DIET IV & SITE

ASSESSMENT

VITALS	NEURO	RESP
	CARDIO	GI
	GU	MUSCULOSKELETAL
Na Glucose K WBC Mg Hgb Ca Hct Ph Plt Cr PT/INR BUN Other	SKIN	PSYCH

RECOMMENDATIONS

PLAN OF CARE	TO-DO LIST	PATIENT EDUCATION

MEDICATION LIST

GENERIC NAME: **BRAND NAME:**
DOSE: ROUTE: DRUG CLASS:
INDICATION(S): NOTES:

GENERIC NAME: **BRAND NAME:**
DOSE: ROUTE: DRUG CLASS:
INDICATION(S): NOTES:

GENERIC NAME: **BRAND NAME:**
DOSE: ROUTE: DRUG CLASS:
INDICATION(S): NOTES:

GENERIC NAME: **BRAND NAME:**
DOSE: ROUTE: DRUG CLASS:
INDICATION(S): NOTES:

GENERIC NAME: **BRAND NAME:**
DOSE: ROUTE: DRUG CLASS:
INDICATION(S): NOTES:

GENERIC NAME: **BRAND NAME:**
DOSE: ROUTE: DRUG CLASS:
INDICATION(S): NOTES:

GENERIC NAME: **BRAND NAME:**
DOSE: ROUTE: DRUG CLASS:
INDICATION(S): NOTES:

GENERIC NAME: **BRAND NAME:**
DOSE: ROUTE: DRUG CLASS:
INDICATION(S): NOTES:

GENERIC NAME: **BRAND NAME:**
DOSE: ROUTE: DRUG CLASS:
INDICATION(S): NOTES:

GENERIC NAME: **BRAND NAME:**
DOSE: ROUTE: DRUG CLASS:
INDICATION(S): NOTES:

GENERIC NAME: **BRAND NAME:**
DOSE: ROUTE: DRUG CLASS:
INDICATION(S): NOTES:

GENERIC NAME: **BRAND NAME:**
DOSE: ROUTE: DRUG CLASS:
INDICATION(S): NOTES:

CARE PLAN

ASSESSMENT

SUBJECTIVE DATA:

OBJECTIVE DATA:

NURSING DIAGNOSIS

PROBLEM(S):

ETIOLOGY:

SIGNS AND SYMPTOMS:

PLANNING

GOAL:

DESIRED (MEASURABLE) OUTCOME:

IMPLEMENTATION

INTERVENTIONS:

EVALUATION

OUTCOME:

EVIDENCED BY:

NOTES

SBAR (PATIENT OVERVIEW)

SITUATION

ROOM NAME AGE/SEX CODE ADMIT DATE	DIAGNOSIS MD/CONSULTS ALLERGIES

BACKGROUND

MEDICAL HISTORY	FALL RISK PRECAUTIONS ISOLATION DIET IV & SITE

ASSESSMENT

VITALS	NEURO	RESP
	CARDIO	GI
	GU	MUSCULOSKELETAL
Na Glucose K WBC Mg Hgb Ca Hct Ph Plt Cr PT/INR BUN Other	SKIN	PSYCH

RECOMMENDATIONS

PLAN OF CARE	TO-DO LIST	PATIENT EDUCATION

MEDICATION LIST

GENERIC NAME:		**BRAND NAME:**
DOSE:	ROUTE:	DRUG CLASS:
INDICATION(S):	NOTES:	

GENERIC NAME:		**BRAND NAME:**
DOSE:	ROUTE:	DRUG CLASS:
INDICATION(S):	NOTES:	

GENERIC NAME:		**BRAND NAME:**
DOSE:	ROUTE:	DRUG CLASS:
INDICATION(S):	NOTES:	

GENERIC NAME:		**BRAND NAME:**
DOSE:	ROUTE:	DRUG CLASS:
INDICATION(S):	NOTES:	

GENERIC NAME:		**BRAND NAME:**
DOSE:	ROUTE:	DRUG CLASS:
INDICATION(S):	NOTES:	

GENERIC NAME:		**BRAND NAME:**
DOSE:	ROUTE:	DRUG CLASS:
INDICATION(S):	NOTES:	

GENERIC NAME:		**BRAND NAME:**
DOSE:	ROUTE:	DRUG CLASS:
INDICATION(S):	NOTES:	

GENERIC NAME:		**BRAND NAME:**
DOSE:	ROUTE:	DRUG CLASS:
INDICATION(S):	NOTES:	

GENERIC NAME:		**BRAND NAME:**
DOSE:	ROUTE:	DRUG CLASS:
INDICATION(S):	NOTES:	

GENERIC NAME:		**BRAND NAME:**
DOSE:	ROUTE:	DRUG CLASS:
INDICATION(S):	NOTES:	

GENERIC NAME:		**BRAND NAME:**
DOSE:	ROUTE:	DRUG CLASS:
INDICATION(S):	NOTES:	

GENERIC NAME:		**BRAND NAME:**
DOSE:	ROUTE:	DRUG CLASS:
INDICATION(S):	NOTES:	

CARE PLAN

ASSESSMENT

SUBJECTIVE DATA:

OBJECTIVE DATA:

NURSING DIAGNOSIS

PROBLEM(S):

ETIOLOGY:

SIGNS AND SYMPTOMS:

PLANNING

GOAL:

DESIRED (MEASURABLE) OUTCOME:

IMPLEMENTATION

INTERVENTIONS:

EVALUATION

OUTCOME:

EVIDENCED BY:

NOTES

SBAR (PATIENT OVERVIEW)

SITUATION

ROOM NAME AGE/SEX CODE ADMIT DATE	DIAGNOSIS MD/CONSULTS ALLERGIES

BACKGROUND

MEDICAL HISTORY	FALL RISK PRECAUTIONS ISOLATION DIET IV & SITE

ASSESSMENT

VITALS	NEURO	RESP
	CARDIO	GI
	GU	MUSCULOSKELETAL
Na Glucose K WBC Mg Hgb Ca Hct Ph Plt Cr PT/INR BUN Other	SKIN	PSYCH

RECOMMENDATIONS

PLAN OF CARE	TO-DO LIST	PATIENT EDUCATION

MEDICATION LIST

GENERIC NAME: **BRAND NAME:**
DOSE: ROUTE: DRUG CLASS:
INDICATION(S): NOTES:

GENERIC NAME: **BRAND NAME:**
DOSE: ROUTE: DRUG CLASS:
INDICATION(S): NOTES:

GENERIC NAME: **BRAND NAME:**
DOSE: ROUTE: DRUG CLASS:
INDICATION(S): NOTES:

GENERIC NAME: **BRAND NAME:**
DOSE: ROUTE: DRUG CLASS:
INDICATION(S): NOTES:

GENERIC NAME: **BRAND NAME:**
DOSE: ROUTE: DRUG CLASS:
INDICATION(S): NOTES:

GENERIC NAME: **BRAND NAME:**
DOSE: ROUTE: DRUG CLASS:
INDICATION(S): NOTES:

GENERIC NAME: **BRAND NAME:**
DOSE: ROUTE: DRUG CLASS:
INDICATION(S): NOTES:

GENERIC NAME: **BRAND NAME:**
DOSE: ROUTE: DRUG CLASS:
INDICATION(S): NOTES:

GENERIC NAME: **BRAND NAME:**
DOSE: ROUTE: DRUG CLASS:
INDICATION(S): NOTES:

GENERIC NAME: **BRAND NAME:**
DOSE: ROUTE: DRUG CLASS:
INDICATION(S): NOTES:

GENERIC NAME: **BRAND NAME:**
DOSE: ROUTE: DRUG CLASS:
INDICATION(S): NOTES:

GENERIC NAME: **BRAND NAME:**
DOSE: ROUTE: DRUG CLASS:
INDICATION(S): NOTES:

CARE PLAN

ASSESSMENT

SUBJECTIVE DATA:

OBJECTIVE DATA:

NURSING DIAGNOSIS

PROBLEM(S):

ETIOLOGY:

SIGNS AND SYMPTOMS:

PLANNING

GOAL:

DESIRED (MEASURABLE) OUTCOME:

IMPLEMENTATION

INTERVENTIONS:

EVALUATION

OUTCOME:

EVIDENCED BY:

NOTES

Made in United States
Cleveland, OH
22 July 2025